ASTIR

A PUBLISHER'S LIFE-STORY

ASTIR

A PUBLISHER'S LIFE-STORY

BY

JOHN ADAMS THAYER

BOSTON
SMALL, MAYNARD & COMPANY, Publishers
1910

THE UNIVERSITY PRESS, CAMBRIDGE, U. S. A.

To My Wife

CONTENTS

A CONFIDENCE

A CONFIDENCE

AFTER thirty years of hard and unremitting work in the business world, circumstances arose which divorced me from my fulfilled ambitions. The alimony was all-sufficient and I went to live in Paris. There I met many famous men. Talking one day with an author who, though highly successful, produces what the critics agree with the public in calling literature, he said: "You publishers do not pay us ten cents nor five nor even a cent a word for what we write. There is not one of my books of which whole chapters have not been recast three and four times. Pages of manuscript are written, rewritten, then destroyed, to be done afresh. I have worked for days over a few hundred words which would not fill a page of an ordinary book. Writing is work, and the hardest kind of work. The man who digs with pick and shovel in the street has an easy job in comparison."

As I thought over his words I wondered if I, too, could not write a book. I believed I had something to say. If the art of writing came by work and work — and yet more work — there was hope for me. Had I not written and rewritten advertisements till they passed muster, and in the end realized large sums? But an advertisement — while it may be a short story — is rather a distant relation of a book. How should I clothe my ideas to fit them for the polite society in leather and cloth on the world's great bookshelf? I envied the trained writer who, knowing the style of many men — the lucid Howells, the picturesque Gautier, the descriptive Dickens

— could, as I thought, fashion to his own ends the diction that best suited his theme. I know now that a writer, if he is sincere, does not pick this or that style as a printer chooses this or that font of type. Good or bad, it must be as much a part of him as his character.

But this I had to learn, and while I was groping for light, someone told me to read the memoirs of a famous general. At the end of the first chapter I put the book aside, for it told only of ancestors. I have ancestors myself — one, they say, made himself felt in William the Conqueror's day — but their dim ghosts played no part in my world of actualities, and plainly had no business in my book. Disappointed in my general, I decided to tell this story in my own way. Dates and figures, which bore most people, I have avoided. Details I have given when details seemed significant, and old letters and scrapbooks, preserved from boyhood, have repeatedly recalled them with a precision which no memory, however retentive, could equal.

Though it was my good fortune to know some of them intimately, I have not essayed to depict or characterize the employers and co-workers with whom I have touched elbows in my business career. I have merely set down, in all sincerity and without prejudice, a few plain truths, and I trust that the most romancing spirit will see naught else between the lines.

This autobiography is a story of hard work, not luck. To quote an appreciative friend: "When a man starts as a printer and makes a habit of working unlimited hours a day, using every pound of pressure and energy, developing every atom of his originality and initiative, I don't think it particularly lucky if he arrives somewhere at the end of forty odd years. It recalls

Maurice Barrymore's remark at billiards, when he made a twice round the table shot on a fluke, which caused his opponent to drop his cue and exclaim: " Holy God ! " With his sweet smile, Barrymore replied: "No, not wholly God. I was in it, too."

Hard work has entered into these pages, but with the work has come pleasure. To live one's business life over again, as I have here, is a privilege which few know. With the optimism which has been my lifelong tonic, I send this book forth. American youth is ambitious to do something worth while. As I see it, there is but one legitimate road to that goal.

CHAPTER ONE

A Publisher at Thirteen

CHAPTER ONE

A Publisher at Thirteen

HEN as a mere child I went upon the platform at a Sunday School concert and recited:

"When I'm a man, a man, I'll be a printer if I can, and I can,"

I was probably as heedless of the real meaning of the couplet as I was of its prophecy. Led to a seat beside my mother, I sat with my hand in hers and heard the other boys declare, "I'll be a lawyer," and "I'll be a preacher if I can, and I can," with equal unconsciousness that these callings also would figure among my future ambitions. As advertising then ranked as neither art, trade,

3

nor profession, it found no place among these stimulative jingles.

I don't know where I got the idea of becoming a preacher, but I did entertain it. In fact, I have in my scrapbook a twenty-five year old letter from the secretary of the Boston Unitarian Association acknowledging my application for assistance, and promising its serious consideration. The matter went little further, however. I consulted my dear old friend, Daniel Monroe Wilson, author of the well-known book, " Where Independence Was Born," then pastor of the first Unitarian Church of Quincy, Massachusetts, and I remember that while he did not advise me against entering the ministry, he spoke of the small salaries received by ministers, of his own many charges, and of the difficulties he had met in trying to make his sermons please the important men in the church, and at the same time

4

interest the women. I felt then that I had a " call " to preach, but I have come to doubt its force. Had it been serious, nothing would have stopped me from following my bent. At that period too many young men without funds burned to undertake the cure of souls, but since even the clergy confuse their sources of inspiration it is not surprising that the lay mind often goes astray. It was one of the cloth who in later years told me the story of a brother minister who resigned a charge of many years to accept a parish only ten miles away. " I feel that I am called," he said. A practical member of his vestry inquired what salary the new parish was to pay, and on receiving his answer, dryly remarked: " Dear brother, that is not a call, it 's a raise."

As for the law, that was my father's idea, as was the idea which grew out of it and determined my career. A native

5

of Vermont, my father came in early
manhood to Massachusetts at the time
Sumner, Wilson, and Wendell Phillips
were spurring people to think about the
great issues which had their final settlement in the War of the Rebellion. He
took an active interest in the problems
of labor, abolition, and currency reform
and became known as a man of sterling
principle, fearless speech, and as an un-
compromising opponent of slavery. My
mother's interest in these matters was
no less keen. She had early developed
a talent for writing, and even as a girl
had been, with Lucy Larcom and Mary
Livermore, a contributor to that once
famous journal of her birthplace, "The
Lowell Offering." In later life she wrote
much for the local papers of Cambridge,
the "Boston Commonwealth," and "The
Woman's Journal;" while the "Christian
Leader" contained weekly contributions

6

from her, both prose and poetry. Of such parentage, I was born in Boston, February 20, 1861, two weeks before the inauguration of Abraham Lincoln, and received my father's name. Several horoscopes, given me for my amusement in after years, agree that on that date Mars and Jupiter were in friendly juxtaposition, and therefore I could be considered lucky. So I have been considered, but inasmuch as for twenty years after my schooldays my lot consisted of hard work at long hours for small pay, I have concluded that luck, as Matthew Arnold said of genius, is largely a question of energy. I am willing to concede, however, that it was a piece of good fortune to begin life in a community which from colonial times downwards has smelled of printer's ink. This local characteristic had beyond doubt its influence in shaping that second idea of my father's which I mentioned at the

7

top of this long paragraph. His future lawyer must have an education, and realizing that the "printing art," as he called it, was a great educator, he purchased for me in my thirteenth year a small printing press and a few fonts of type.

I began by printing calling cards at ten to twenty cents a dozen, and as it was then a fad for young people to exchange them, I soon put money in my purse. Within a year I had made enough to buy a small foot-power press, and by adding to my fonts of type, I was able to print business cards and do other modest commercial jobs. My ambition outran this little success, however, and I launched a four-page monthly paper about four by six inches in size. I called this pygmy "The Printer," and at the head of the editorial column styled myself "Editor and Publisher." Under the caption "Terms" one might further read that the paper was

8

to be had for ten cents a year, a prudent stipulation adding that the annual postage, which amounted to twelve cents, was to be paid by the subscriber. The advertising rates were as tempting as the price of subscription. Three cents would purchase a line of Long Primer or what is now known as ten-point — I had no Agate; while fifteen cents would insure a whole inch of publicity placed beside "pure" reading. But, as for securing advertising, I recall no precocious signs of fitness for the business I was eventually to follow. Such as I obtained was chiefly taken on the "exchange" basis, and some fruit, candy, or a bunch of mild cigarettes, for strictly private consumption, would in a twinkling exhaust the earnings of an inch of space. My real profits were indirect. I picked up, self-taught, the rudiments of a valuable trade, and I absorbed enough of the "lead poisoning of type," to borrow Oliver

9

Wendell Holmes' phrase, to color my whole future. "Keep on, John," said Charles Walker, superintendent of the famous Riverside Press, from whom I used to buy scrap paper for my diminutive monthly; "some day you will be the head of a publishing house as big as this."

Meanwhile I shared the usual pastimes of the American schoolboy. For us Cambridge lads there was swimming in the Charles at an old dilapidated fort called the "magazine," some boating, and an occasional excursion across the bridge to the Beacon Park race course in Brighton.

We did not sit in the grand stand. A few of us knew a secret passage under a corner of the fence, which for a number of seasons escaped the vigilance of the guardians of the Park. The best race I thus saw was the one in which Goldsmith Maid trotted a mile in 2.14, the record at that time. If there were no races, we boys would ourselves make trials of speed for a quarter of a mile or more. One of my companions was John Clarkson, who afterwards gained celebrity as a baseball pitcher. He was then, in fact, the pitcher of a club called the "Centennials," which I captained. One match game with a Boston club I can never forget. Both pitchers were excellent, and at the end of the fifth inning neither side had made a run. The "Centennials" were on the outfield, Clarkson had struck out two men, and excitement ran high. My position at this critical juncture was that of catcher, and as gloves and masks were expensive, our club did not possess them. The upshot of this enforced economy was disastrous for me. Clarkson's next ball was a foul tip, and as he already had much of the speed for which he was celebrated later, it shot through my hands and, striking my

mouth, knocked me down. Obliged to go
to a neighboring house for repairs, I found
on my return that our opponents had made
three runs. I was able to resume my place,
however, and as the rival pitcher lacked
Clarkson's staying power, the Boston
Club went home defeated. I bear with
me yet, unnoticed by the world, some
results of that, to me, famous game of
ball.

As for my education, in the literal sense
of the word, it was sound so far as it
went. I was graduated from the Webster
Grammar School and attended the High
School for about a month. Many a time
since I have wished that I could have continued, for it is this latter training, even
more, perhaps, than a college course,
which is the young man's mainstay when
he enters business. But my people were
poor, a livelihood had to be gained, and
so it fell out that the composing room

became my high school and the world my
university.

I sought work in a printing office as a
matter of course. It was the natural thing
to do. I had not only handled my own
type; I had almost all my boyhood neigh-
bored and had the freedom of the Riverside
Press. Knowing the superintendent and
many of the workers, I had become familiar
with every branch of the business. Thus
it was that I found my first employment,
not as an office boy, but as a bona fide
printer. My pay was five dollars a week;
my hours were from seven to six.

The story of the next five years may be
briefly told. It was a struggle to rise by
shifting from one printing office to another.
Sometimes a change would mean slightly
more pay; or again, the same wage with
a better opportunity to master the business.
So it was that in those five years I worked
in seven different places, and thereby

gained invaluable experience, for practically every printing office has its distinct line of work. For example, with my first employer, Daniel Dwyer, of Sudbury Street, Boston, I got my first knowledge of newspaper work, for he printed "The Daily Hotel Reporter," a paper which chronicled the hotel arrivals, the weather probabilities, and information of like value. The weather report came late, and as in those days there was only an hourly horse car to Cambridge, the tardy item often compelled me to choose between a tedious wait for the pottering car or a walk home. Many a night, as I tramped over the Charles, I kept myself awake by singing "I stood on the bridge at midnight," but though it was the same old bridge of Longfellow's song, the clocks somehow always struck a later hour.

The poet himself was an occasional visitor to the composing room of one of

14

my places of employment. This was the University Press in Cambridge, the oldest printing establishment in America and the home of many famous books. I recall that I worked on a new edition of "Uncle Tom's Cabin" among others, and it was, of course, his own volumes which brought Longfellow's snowy locks and beard amidst our dingy toil. Of charming personality, and a manner at once dignified and sweet, it was a pleasure to the workmen even to see him, while to have a word with him in reference to a piece of his work in hand was counted a great honor.

Changing from shop to shop as I did puzzled my friends. It made it difficult for them to keep track of me, and it also caused them to believe that there was something radically wrong in my makeup. Yet during these migrations my salary increased by successive stages till at nineteen I held a permanent situation at twelve dollars a week, with a prospect of a small advance. But I was too ambitious to be content with this, and having heard much of the success of a few young men who had followed Horace Greeley's historic advice, I decided to throw up my position and go to Chicago, which meant West to me. It conveyed another meaning to my fellow workers in the printing office, however. They had planned to give me a bowie knife and a revolver, but on learning that I was only going to Chicago, decided that I would need nothing of the kind, and presented me with their good wishes instead.

I remember distinctly the day I went down to draw my last week's salary. The leading member of the firm looked over his glasses kindly, but not sympathetically, and said:

"So you are going to Chicago, are you?"

"Yes," I replied.

"Have you a job out there?"

"No."

"Well," he said, "I guess you'll get one; you've a good trade. But remember 'A rolling stone gathers no moss.'"

17

CHAPTER TWO

A Union Printer

CHAPTER TWO

A Union Printer

T this time trade unionism was not deeply rooted in Boston. So lax, in fact, was its grip that members of the Typographical Union were allowed, if they chose, to work at a lower wage than the fixed scale of fifteen dollars a week. In Chicago the situation was far different, and before I started West I was strongly urged by one of my fellow workmen to join the union in Boston, and obtain a traveling card, permitting me to work in all offices throughout the country. As this implied a jump from twelve to eighteen dollars a week, the prevailing scale in Chicago, I

lent a willing ear. But on looking into
the question of eligibility I found the con-
stitution prescribed that a union printer
must be twenty-one at least, and have
worked as many years as an apprentice as
love-sick Jacob first agreed to serve for
Rachel. It seemed to me that I had run
against a dead wall, but my friend re-
assured me by saying, that although I
was only nineteen, my knowledge of the
business was such that he felt warranted
in arranging the matter for me, which
he did.

Thus equipped, I began a journey
which etched itself on my memory as
many of far greater scope have not.
For one thing, I had my first and only
ride on an engine, an experience I have
never yearned to repeat, as the engineer
derived more amusement from me than
I did from his hospitality. The Grand
Trunk Railway, by which I went on

account of its low fare, quite upheld its inglorious reputation. There were countless delays, an accident to the engine, and a loss of nearly a day in the schedule, but arrive we did at last and I began my hunt for work. The value of my traveling card was at once made plain. Within two or three days after I reached Chicago I found employment at the union scale.

Unfortunately, the disadvantage of union membership also developed. My position was temporary, the dull season came, and I found myself in the street, handicapped by the local prohibition against accepting less than the standard wage. The work was there. Again and again during those weeks of idleness I could have had it. At last I came across a most tempting opening. A foremanship in an office publishing a number of educational papers offered a kind of experience which had not previously come my way. It was not a union

23

shop, however, and its pay fell two dollars short of the prescribed scale. I decided that the situation was desperate and needed a desperate remedy. But what? Long pondering persuaded me to appeal to authority against the cast-iron rule.

Acting on this idea, I called on the secretary of the Typographical Union, and was by him passed along to the chairman of some forgotten committee, whom I found in the composing room of the "Inter-ocean" making up the paper for the day. In this forum I pleaded my case. I was out of work; I needed money; if I could have permission to accept this lower wage until another opportunity came, I would not only relieve my necessity, but keep a "rat" out of a job. I think this latter argument must have struck him as new. "Rats," as non-union men were called, were not regarded with favor in Chicago, and as I

24

waxed eloquent on the wisdom of exclud-
ing them from work, I perceived that my
court of appeal was duly impressed. The
permit was granted and I took the coveted
place till the dull season passed.

The fact that I was now for the first
time a foreman impressed me but little,
for, bound as I was to keep my promise
to secure union work as soon as possible,
I knew my authority would be brief.
The value of this stop-gap lay in the
character of the shop itself, which bore
out my father's belief that the printing art
was a great educator. This office was
different from any of my former places,
and the various educational books, papers,
and pamphlets which flowed from its
presses gave me at once an insight into
the care one must expend on work of this
kind and widened my notion of my calling.
In the popular fancy a printer is an ink-
smudged pressman, or a compositor who

sticks the type of a book or daily newspaper; but just as there are many branches
of the business, so there are many kinds
of printers. Used in its broad and proper
sense, the term "printer" means much,
and brings to mind not only the names of
men like Gutenberg, Caxton, and Franklin, but a whole train of reflection on the
force which the art they practiced has
exerted upon human history. Taking the
rank it did, the shop of my temporary
foremanship could not fail to influence a
youth eager to get on, but besides the
benefit I had from the character of its
output, I enjoyed the special advantage
of frequent talks with the cultivated
gentleman who held the chair of editor.
On publication day the last hour before
going to press was usually devoted to
changing words in particular passages,
and this hour the editor would spend
with me. To this day I marvel at the

ease with which this expert would trace words back to their original source that he might use the ones which most authoritatively expressed his thought.

The slack season over, I readily found work with the J. M. W. Jones Company, one of the largest printing offices of that period. Here again was another phase of the business. They called themselves railroad printers, and although they also handled poster and job work, the printing of rate books, coupon tickets, thousand-mile books, and the like was their principal feature. Few things could be more tedious. For a fortnight I saturated my brain with U P, D & R G, C B & Q, C & A, P R R, etc., as I set up a route book for the use of ticket agents throughout the country. Seeing no glimmer of progress ahead of me in this sad stuff, I chose an opportune time to buttonhole the foreman and tell him of my training for the higher

27

forms of job work. This means the typography of letterheads, booklets, invitations, and such orders from manuscript copy, and is a class of work which barely one out of a hundred ordinary compositors can perform. Owing to the illness of one of the men, I was given a trial, and acquitting myself satisfactorily, I was retained in preference to many employees of longer service, who were laid off when dull times again came round.

In this office I participated in my only strike. Conducted with admirable dignity, it vividly impressed me at the time, and I think deserves mention here. I have already pointed out that the Typographical Union in Chicago was a powerful organization. Each large printing office had a "chapel," so called, and whenever a local difficulty of any sort arose, the chairman had merely to say the word and the matter would be discussed on the spot. One

28

afternoon there came to my ears the same
sound Mr. Speaker makes when he calls
the House of Representatives to order. It
was the chairman of our chapel. He had
no gavel, but his liberal use of a mallet on
the marble slab, found in all printing offices
for the imposition of type pages, brought
us flocking round him instantly. When
all the hundred or more compositors were
assembled, he said that a number of members had requested him to call a special
meeting, and with this brief preface asked
a compositor named Cummings to state
the case. Mr. Cummings was also brief.
''There are few men here," he said, ''who
are satisfied with the present foreman. I
don't question his ability as a printer or his
efficiency as an executive. The volume of
work he turns out daily is immense. Unfortunately, the volume of his profanity is
also immense. We have made complaints,
but the truth is he can no more change his

29

foul speech and hectoring manner than the leopard can change his spots. We are men, not slaves, and I know I only voice the general opinion of my fellow workmen when I say that this office needs a new head. As we have previously brought this matter to the attention of the general superintendent without result, I move that we quit this office in a body and do not return until another foreman is appointed from among the employees of this room." The resolution was carried unanimously, and changing quietly to our street clothes, we departed. We all returned the next morning. There was a new foreman.

The change in executive made no difference to me. Handling my own work with dispatch, I had come in for none of the deposed foreman's profanity, while I flattered myself that I had entrenched myself in a position which I could have as long as I liked. But with this conviction came

30

the query: Where will it lead? A foremanship would be the next step, after long
service; then an office of my own, which
would require capital. I decided that if I
meant some day to be my own master it
behooved me to acquaint myself with the
business end of printing, and with this in
view I one morning took off my apron and
presented myself to the superintendent.
In a little speech, which I had carefully
prepared beforehand, I told him that I had
had wide experience in artistic job work
and knew, if he would transfer me to his
business department that, on account of my
ability to sketch and plan, I could give
ideas to customers which would increase
orders. I also added, when he asked what
salary I wanted, that though I now drew
the usual composing-room wage of eighteen
dollars, I was perfectly willing to work for
twelve dollars until I had proved myself
worth more. The superintendent listened

31

to me patiently throughout, promised to consider the matter — and probably forgot all about it. Having then little of the persistency which I later found it necessary to develop, I made no second call upon him, but continued in the room above till after about a year's absence the incessant hot weather joined forces with a fit of homesickness to drive me back to my parents, my friends, and the salt breezes I knew so well how to find in a sailboat in Boston Harbor.

The foreman yielded a very reluctant assent to this vacation project of mine. In fact, his last word was a charge to hurry back and give the other boys a chance. The knowledge and experience I had gained in the West proved of such value, however, that I secured a Boston foremanship at a Chicago salary. Thus another year passed. More experience came with it, of course, but no real prog-

32

ress towards my ideals, and I therefore
accepted the offer of a New Bedford
printer who wanted a foreman. This
man cherished a dream of starting a
daily newspaper as soon as conditions
should warrant the venture, but the
scheme hung fire in my time, and the
close of a year in his employ again
found me ripe for change. I was and
have ever been a stout heretic regard-
ing the rolling stone adage, which my
old-time employer tagged to his sober
godspeed for Chicago. Moss is for
ruins. In change lie possibilities.

It was at this juncture that I had my
first real experience in soliciting advertising. The week before I left New
Bedford there appeared in one of the
daily papers three columns of taking
description of various local enterprises.
It belonged in what is known as the
" reading notice" category. In reality

33

an advertisement, it read like news. I thought the language used was worthy of a better cause, but the scheme itself interested me, for, happening to meet the man who controlled it, he talked to me of his methods and of the towns he had "worked." His first move, on arriving in a promising field, was to engage a column or two of space in one of the leading dailies at advertising rates. He would then call upon the chief firms, advertisers or non-advertisers, and presenting his newly printed card inscribed "Special Editorial Writer" to the paper in which for the time being he owned space, would confide his intention to fill two or three columns of Saturday's issue with live editorial comment upon the foremost business houses of the town. He would state that a big announcement was not necessary, the smaller the paragraph the better, and

34

then, if an order were given him, gravely
note the personnel of the establishment,
the date of its founding, and its speciality.
By evening these memoranda would re-
appear in an item of irresistible praise.
If a merchant said he would take twenty
lines, the paragraph would fill forty,
so cleverly dovetailed that to eliminate
half would ruin all. Naturally, the labor
of writing amounted to nothing after this
self-styled editor and his assistants had
covered a number of cities. If an item
were needed for a florist, say, they had
only to turn to an indexed book to find a
flowery paragraph which had already done
good service.

This man's account of his success led
me to believe that advertising, then in
its infancy, was something it might be
well to add to my fund of practical experience. In any event, it promised a
living while I looked about for another

35

stepping-stone. So reasoning, I invaded Rhode Island and worked the editorial advertising scheme with the "Providence Times." I took two young men with me, advancing their traveling expenses on the understanding that they should reimburse me out of the profits from their work. My assistants, however, showed no aptitude for soliciting orders. Having paid down a deposit for space, the work had to be pushed to completion, but as I did practically all of it myself, meanwhile footing the bills for three, my personal gain was small. Indeed, I even worked one night on the "Times" as a compositor to add five dollars to my funds. The publisher of the paper congratulated me on filling so much space at a time when advertising was languid, and even debated offering me a position as solicitor, but nothing came of it. Nor did anything

36

come of my round of the printing offices. There was but one offer made me which seemed worth a second thought. This was from a master printer who wished to give up active work. I was to manage his place for a year, and then, taking it over myself, pay him out of the profits. The plant had been successful, but as I looked over the office, with its dark corners and low-studded walls, I contrasted it with the large well-lighted composing rooms to which I had been accustomed, and there and then told myself it was no place to spend my life. With this decision, more momentous than I knew, I again set my face towards Boston.

CHAPTER THREE

TYPEFOUNDING BEFORE THE TRUST

CHAPTER THREE

Typefounding before the Trust

OSTON seemed to be my Mecca. It did not worry me that I was going back without a position. I had my trade and the Typographical Union here would not require me to work at a specified wage. By now, however, I had the fixed idea that the printing business and I should part company, and I decided to advertise for a place in a publishing house or some kindred business in which my previous experience would tell.

An opening turned up. Calling at the Boston Type Foundry, I learned to my delight that there was a possibility of a few weeks' service in the specimen department. Delight! The word is not half strong enough. To give a job compositor free rein in a typefoundry is like turning a youngster loose in a toy shop. Brimful of enthusiasm, I presented myself to Mr. John K. Rogers, who, though he bore in print the unusual title "Agent," was the actual head and largest owner of this solid house which traced its beginnings back to the administration of President Madison. He was a Bostonian of the old school, dignified, courteous, amiable, and so considerate of others that he hesitated to let me take this temporary work because he thought it might cost me a permanent position elsewhere. My eagerness overcame his scruples, however, and I was engaged at the same, unescapable salary of eighteen dollars a week for a term, as he carefully explained, not exceeding three weeks, the hours being from eight to five. This was my first encounter with the eight-hour plan, and I showed my surprise.

"I long ago decided," he said jestingly, "that the proper division of time is eight hours for work, eight hours for play, eight hours for sleep — "

"And eight dollars a day?" I continued, completing the rhyme.

"Not yet, young man," he smiled. "Not yet."

I think I would have worked for eight cents a day rather than forego the toy shop. The first days were full of surprises. Great novelties to me were the types for the blind, and the Hawaiians, both of which were exclusive products of this foundry. It was a wonder, too, where all the type went to, for over a thousand pounds were cast and finished every day. But this was before the Mergenthaler typesetting machine revolutionized methods, and while country weeklies would use their outfits for a decade or more, the big dailies, issuing many editions and printing from stereotype plates on rotary presses, required a new "dress" every second year. Neither the hydraulic hot press nor the later cold press had been introduced, and stereotyping from papier-mâché matrices was generally in vogue, the matrix being prepared in the old-fashioned way by beating the paper into the type form with brushes. One famous newspaper, the "Salem News," was still printed directly from the type on a curved rotary press, and many was the paragraph which, through hasty "justification," spilled out while the press was running. Conditions being such, outfits of body and job letter were always being shipped to the papers of New England, and their supply was an important factor in the business.

But the most profitable branch of type-founding then, as now, was the manufacture of "job" faces, used for headings,

44

newspaper advertisements, and, more especially, circulars, business cards, letter-heads, and the like. Fresh designs were from time to time brought out by the various typefounders, and when I entered the Boston establishment three new series of letters were ready to be shown to printers. It was amusing to discover one of the oldest tricks of trade in general playing its part in the sale of these wares. Just as the fruit vender always puts the largest and rosiest apples at the top, so the typefounder selects certain plump capitals to grace his specimen sheet and keeps others out of sight. There were less than twenty letters in our alphabet. A F L P T W and Y were avoided, but M, considered the most perfect, was chosen as the "monitor," and all the other letters had to line with it.

Two imaginary signboards

JOHN ROBINSON — HIDES
WILLIAM LATHAM — PAPER
45

best illustrate the typefounder's discreet arrangement of his apple cart.

As I studied the specimen sheets which had hitherto been issued to display new type faces, I perceived why Mr. Rogers felt sure that he needed my services for only three weeks. But I forgot the time limit. I saw an opportunity and I felt I was equal to it. Why not show these different faces in a manner so attractive and unusual that printers would not glance and pass by, but grow absorbed and decide that they could not do without them? On my way home from my second day's work I bought two bottles of colored ink — red and green — some paste and a ruler, and with the printed samples of type before me, I worked far into the night, preparing a proposed specimen sheet, to be printed in colors. Previously these had shown merely two or three sample lines and then left it to the printer's imagination — if he had one — to discover how the type could best be used. My sheet gave not only samples, but adequate illustrations.

Taking my night's work to the foundry, I showed it to my sole associate of the specimen department, a pressman. He thought it novel and admirable, but doubted if I could put the scheme through. More valuable was his suggestion that I delay broaching the subject till after lunch, a piece of advice capable of wide application. The early afternoon is the time to take any new suggestion to any employer. Approaching Mr. Rogers, therefore, when the important affairs of the morning were off his mind and the small bottle of claret he drank daily was still a warm and cheering memory, I found him not only pleased with the interest I had taken, but even willing as soon as I made it plain that it was no more difficult, if one knew how, to print in colors than in black, to give me authority to go ahead. It thus fell out that the third day of my employment saw me in charge of the specimen department, consisting of one man, one press, and, most important, types and materials for my every want.

This foothold obtained, I worked with an aim more far-reaching than the sale of this particular series of type. I wanted this specimen sheet to coax such prompt and liberal orders from the printers as should prove the value of my idea and remind my employer that he had other fine faces of type, too gingerly shown in the past, which I could also display in an attractive manner. On the day the sheets were mailed I took care that the foreman of every large printing office in the city should personally receive a copy. The result was all I hoped. Orders flowed in at once, the three-week limit was passed

48

in safety, and plans for new sheets and new specimen books multiplied so fast that I saw myself a fixture for as long as I chose to remain.

With the assurance of permanency came the same old query: " Where will it lead?" A rolling stone who had profited by nearly every roll, I could never settle into an easy corner and forget the thought of advancement. It seemed to me now that, with my knowledge, I could help both the business and myself if I were to see the printers personally, as a sales-man, but my employer vetoed the idea. Another suggestion, which I still believe sound, also failed to appeal to him. There were in St. Louis two foundries: one the St. Louis Type Foundry, the other the Central Type Foundry, once a branch of our own house, but now a separate concern manufacturing both faces and type bodies identical with those of the

49

parent establishment. It struck me that if we could arrange with the former firm to keep a consignment of our faces in stock, we should have a new outlet in the Southwest for Boston-made type. It must be remembered that these were the days when the type bodies of the foundries differed one from another so widely that it was the part of wisdom for a printer to deal exclusively with a single house. These various bodies of type, known under the arbitrary nomenclature of "Nonpareil," "Long Primer," "Pica," and other names as unmeaning to the layman, were done away with by mutual agreement even before the Type Trust came into being, so that now the type bodies of all American, and even the English foundries, are on a basis of "points." Framed to deal with the haphazard condition of things before the point system, my plan had a value which

would, I think, have justified itself in
practice, but the conservatism of both the
Boston and St. Louis foundries was such
that nothing came of it except the conviction on my part that it was time for me
to try another field. Thinking that perhaps one of the large English firms might
be susceptible to American ideas, I wrote to
the two leading typefoundries of London.
The reply from the Caslon Type Foundry
was novel and gave a piece of good advice.
"Whilst thanking you for the offer of
your services," it ran, "we beg to say
that, in our opinion, it is better for a
young man to remain in a country where
labor is, and is likely to be for some
time, at a premium, than to go to an old
country where labor is, and is likely to
be for some time, at a discount."

The immediate cause of my leaving
the Boston Type Foundry was a patent
hammer, one of the inventions of my

father. This particular hammer, which I now undertook to manufacture, was an improvement upon an earlier model which had been put successfully on the market some twelve years before. This later attempt was less fortunate. Technical difficulties arose, and in less than a year the cost of production had swallowed not only the profits from the sales, but $1200 of borrowed money besides. Boston being glutted already, I set out with a trunk full of hammers for Chicago, but as my arrival coincided with the annual stock taking of the hardware stores, I could as easily have sold parasols to the Eskimos.

Once more I fell back on my trade. Turning up next morning at the printing office where I had been employed so many years before, I found the foreman to be a fellow workman of the days of the profanity strike. With a brief summary of my fortunes in the intervening years, I told him that I wanted, at once, three or four weeks' work.

"All right," he said. "Will you begin now or to-morrow morning?"

I took off my coat.

CHAPTER FOUR

On the Road from Texas to Maine

CHAPTER FOUR

On the Road from Texas to Maine

THIS return to my old trade I determined should be but a makeshift. During the following week I therefore wrote the chief typefounders of the West, applying for a position as salesman. I told of my work with the Boston Type Foundry, and enclosed a copy of a letter given me by Mr. Rogers which contained a sentence I felt sure would catch the eye. This testimonial, as old-time in its flavor as its author, ran: "I believe that Mr. Thayer's ability and honorable conduct entitle him to a more prominent place in the business world." From the St. Louis Type Foundry came a favorable

57

response. They were in need of a man to travel in Texas, but naturally wished to see him in the flesh before coming to terms. Disposing of my hammers to one of the big hardware stores — which ten years later still had them on sale — I said good-bye to my trade for the last time, and took train for St. Louis.

Face to face, the matter was soon arranged. I was to cover Texas and Arkansas, with expenses paid, at a salary larger than I had previously received. The prospect exhilarated me. The eighteen-dollar-a-week mark was finally passed; I could "roll" to my heart's content. As the firm not only manufactured type, machinery, and other printers' supplies, but dealt largely in paper, I spent a preliminary fortnight wandering round the great establishment studying the latter business, of which I knew little. By the end of a week I had memorized the various classifi-

58

cations and could with my eyes shut tell the difference between machine sized and book paper, or No. 1 and No. 2 news. Prices were high in those days and the dailies paid six cents a pound for paper which now costs less than two.

My maiden trip was to last four months, and the program of the first two weeks had been mapped out in minute detail. Midsummer notwithstanding, I was supposed in this space of time to visit several places in Arkansas, and then, crossing the Texas border, make eighteen or twenty towns and cities on the exact days specified in my strenuous itinerary. I found it novel, interesting — and hot. Despite its name, Hot Springs, Arkansas, proved cool, but once in Texas I sighed for the sea breezes and invigorating nights of the East. I thought of the East, too, as I now ran squarely against the Color Line. One piping Sunday in New Boston, when the mercury had climbed to 105° in the shade of the hotel piazza, where, book in hand, I waited for evening, a negro approached, and halting at a respectful distance, asked for a drink of water. "Of course," I said. "Go back to the rear of the house." But I had scarcely taken up my book again when "Get out of here, you black trash! There ain't no water here for such as you!" came explosively from the proprietor's wife, and the negro shot by. The poor wretch was out of sight before intercession was possible, and I could only wonder what my abolitionist parents in the other Boston would think of such a refusal on such a day.

It was perhaps unfair to judge Texas by Eastern standards, however. Life was still rough and chaotic there in many localities. Texarkana, which, as its name implies, owes allegiance to two commonwealths, was the scene of numerous shooting affrays,

60

and one of its notorious saloons stood in
Arkansas so near the state line that a fugi-
tive had merely to cross the street to reach
Texas and absolute immunity till requisition
papers could be obtained. In odd contrast
was the collapsed "boom" town, Denison,
which, once boasting twenty thousand
souls, now reckoned its population by
hundreds. The story of its decline is soon
told : the railroad had failed to come that
way. The factories and fine residences
were tumbling to ruin; the pavements
were grass-grown and treacherous ; the
lamp-posts had a Pisa Tower incline, and
the inhabitants, neither rural nor urban,
were, for lack of a police force, compelled
to take turns in patrolling the silent
streets.

The lot of a salesman in such a country
had little variety and less ease. I used no
Pullman cars. A few were in use on the
"Cannon-Ball" trains, but they were

not for me. When night overtook me on the road, I curled up in the seats of an ordinary day coach with one valise for a foot rest, the other for a pillow. Traveling thus, it will surprise no one that my expenses averaged only two dollars and a half a day. Once when I spent nearly twice that amount I explained my extravagance in the weekly report sent to headquarters. Under the heading ''Remarks'' I wrote : '' The large expense on this day was occasioned by the fact that I left Waco at four in the morning, saw our customers in Temple and Belton, and arrived at Georgetown the next morning at three.'' Valuable experience came with the hardships, however ; my persistence developed, my knowledge of human nature broadened. I bent all my energy towards obtaining orders from responsible firms, and the harder the nut to crack the more pleasure I took in dragging it from its shell. In

Galveston, to give an illustration, the principal publishers greeted me with the statement that they made all their purchases in New York and that I could sell them nothing. Why should they buy of me when the freight rate direct to New York by steamer was less than half that to St. Louis by rail? Nevertheless, when I left town two days later, one of the best orders of my whole trip stood in their name.

This showing so satisfied the firm that they straightway packed me off on another campaign. On this second trip I added much to my knowledge of selling goods, learned much also about traveling salesmen, and made up my mind, if I ever got back, that Texas should see me no more. To bring the company to agree with me was another thing, as I recognized, perhaps a week after my next return to St. Louis, when I was told to get my samples

ready because the Old Man — meaning the
president, William Bright — intended to
start me off again at once. Mr. Bright,
be it said, was no ordinary man. An
indefatigable worker, whose one defect
was a too close attention to detail, he
brought to the direction of this capacity
a mind fertile in ideas. Beyond question
he invented the card index system for
bookkeepers. The ledger of our entire
business was kept on cards arranged
alphabetically in special tin boxes patented
by him, a rod and a padlock securing each
file in the manner now widely known.
Fortunately for me, our personal relations
were of the pleasantest. Often his guest
at luncheon, and a frequent visitor at his
country house, I met an indulgent, if
astonished hearing, when without mincing
words I announced that I had decided to
travel in Texas no more. Asked for
reasons, I furnished many, but the heavy

shot was this: "I intend to marry some day," I said, "and I owe it to my future wife—whom I haven't met—not to become a confirmed traveling man, unable to do anything else, and saddled, perhaps, with bad habits." To the head of a family as happy as it was numerous, this domestic argument made its prompt appeal, and he inquired kindly what I meant to do. I modestly suggested that he permit me to try city trade, a field in which we had no one, and the novelty of the idea taking his fancy, a city salesman I became. A year of such service followed. Then, choosing an opportune time, I asked him if he did not think I was entitled to a better salary. He hesitated for a moment before he answered. "Don't be in a hurry, boy," he said, looking benevolently over his glasses. "There's George, and Ernest, and Frank, who have grown up with me. If I raise your salary, I feel that I must

65

raise theirs." I did not see the logic of this reasoning, and soon after transferred my allegiance to a brass foundry.

This move proving as ill-judged as my experiment with patent hammers, I thereupon committed an even greater error than leaving the typefoundry: I went back to it. The end of another year found me still marking time.

It was a home letter, telling how much I was needed by my parents in their old age, which gave a final spur to my unrest, and I began to cast about for ways and means to return. Learning that with the death of Mr. Rogers the old Boston Type Foundry had passed into the control of its former St. Louis branch, I proposed myself as a salesman for my former house. A new specimen book of the combined faces of both firms was just then under consideration, and my offer to take this over as well clinched the matter, and I

66

was engaged forthwith. My expenses paid, not for the journey merely, but for the cities I visited en route to see our resident agents, I returned with flying colors. That home-coming remains a touching memory to me, for I then came to appreciate the truth, which many learn too late, that life's real joys lie in doing for others.

My work on the specimen book forbade continuous travel, and as I now mapped my own route, followed no cast-iron itinerary, and made few trips of more than a week's length, I found my journeys far pleasanter than in the Southwest. Hard as they had been, however, the experiences of Texas and Arkansas proved of value, and thanks to their schooling, I sold outfits and dresses to many a crusty printer and publisher of conservative New England. Nowhere, East or West, had I known such an

67

obstinate case as I presently encountered
in that stronghold of odd characters,
Vermont. This opinionated citizen of
Burlington bore a reputation so difficult
that salesmen thought it a waste of time
to cross his threshold. Transferred to
the Dark Ages, he would have built up
a lurid reputation as an ogre. Undis-
mayed by these tales, I went early for
my first call, and finding the publisher
out — as I had hoped — mounted to the
composing room, and with the freemasonry
of an old printer, soon had the confidence
of the foreman. His equipment was as bad
as I expected, and as he unburdened his
troubles, I told him that I meant to see
his employer later, and suggested that we
draw up a memorandum of the type and
material really necessary to his work. As
time sped on the list grew, and finally,
in the hope that I might secure an order
for a small part of the things I had set

68

down, I went below. His mail finished, the Terror sat barricaded by his desk, the cares of the universe wrinkling his brow. A curt nod acknowledged — merely acknowledged—my existence, and his perusal of a newspaper continued. Seating myself near, I waited for him to speak. After fifteen minutes he swung suddenly round in his chair.

"What can I do for you?" he demanded peremptorily.

Tone and remark were alike familiar. I had heard them too often to tremble. Handing him my card, I said that it being my duty to call on the leading publishers of Burlington, I had come to his office earlier in the day, and finding him out, had visited his composing room. As a practical printer, I felt sure I could do something for him.

"What is it?" he snapped.

I produced my list.

69

"Here are the things your foreman thinks he needs."

He merely glanced at it.

"We don't need this," he blustered, but prodded the push button for the foreman.

I was such an interested listener to the dialogue which ensued that they withdrew to finish it out of hearing. The list came back cut in half, but the half was mine. Over the hotel dinner that night I made a present of my method to the other salesmen.

It was at this period I heard of the wonderful commissions given book agents, and while I suspected that selling books must be hard indeed to secure such terms from the publishers, I decided to have a try at it during a two weeks' vacation at Bar Harbor. The book was an attractively illustrated volume about that resort; the commission, equally attractive, was forty per cent. I felt sure that if I could only

70

get at the people who lived in these impos-
ing homes, I should sell many copies, but
occupied, as the colony was, with social
affairs, personal interviews proved impossible, and after two days of rebuffs I fell
back on the vain expedient of sending the
book with an inspired letter. The real
reason for my non-success was the false
pride which is the bane of the immature.
I did not want the fascinating young ladies
of my hotel to think I was a book agent!
One volume only found a purchaser. The
subscription blank I sent to the publisher
was a copy; the original, which I still
retain, bears the signature of James G.
Blaine.

But this was merely by the way. My
real work, in sufficient quantity, lay elsewhere. In addition to the special services
I had contracted to perform, I handled a
large amount of the firm's correspondence,
which, neglected by the manager, who held

his place by virtue of family ties, would frequently fall to me. I did not resent this. Active and full of energy, I even took pleasure in attacking a mass of orders, telegrams, and letters a foot high, writing everything by hand. Many a night I would go to the office, work till two o'clock, drop in at the old Boston Tavern for a few hours' sleep, and then return early to my desk. I learned much of business methods in this way, but I could not lift my salary above twenty-five dollars a week, though I did piece out my income with expert appraisals of publishers' and printers' fire losses, which, though infrequent, brought me from thirty to fifty dollars a day.

Matters stood thus when, in 1891, there came persistent rumors that the type-foundries of the country proposed to enter a trust backed by English capital. This was absorbing news for me. If the old Boston Type Foundry were submerged,

72

what sort of life preserver would I get?
I therefore wrote, without delay, to Mr.
James A. St. John, of St. Louis, who was
the virtual head of our combined houses,
asking the truth about this report and my
own chances for an increased salary. His
reply was not reassuring. Unfamiliar
with the details or the results of my work,
he could promise no advancement till he
had, sometime in the vague future, paid a
visit to Boston ; as for the trust, it looked
to him as if it would go through, in which
case he would no longer be identified with
the business.

Plainly it behooved me to seek pastures
new. Some months before I had tried to
enter a publishing house. The attempt
had failed, but the belief remained that
such a business held great possibilities for
a man of my practical knowledge, and I
was even now studying how best to obtain
recognition when I saw an advertisement

73

in the "Boston Herald." It was not a "want ad.," so called. Displayed in large type and occupying three inches of prominent space, it spoke to me as emphatically as if it called me by name.

WANTED
A FIRST-CLASS MAN

To take charge of the advertising pages, make up and direct artistic composition, etc. Must be familiar with the whole range of advertising business, and something of an expert at devising artistic display. — "The Ladies' Home Journal," Boston Office, Temple Place.

I read and reread that advertisement as a street car bore me to Cambridge, and with every reading the conviction grew that here at last was the field for which all my varied experience had been a preparation. There would be many answers, of course. How could I make my own

74

effective? Calling at the Boston office of the "Journal," I learned that only written applications would be received, and that night was devoted to the all-important letter. This I next day supplemented by three other letters written for me by prominent Bostonians who knew my qualifications. One was from Mr. Robert Luce, the author and legislator; another from Mr. Potter, then publisher of "The New England Magazine," who told of his satisfaction with the type I had selected for him without consultation; while the third was from my boyhood encourager and lifelong friend, Charles Walker, superintendent of the Riverside Press. Taking care to have my application typewritten, I thereupon dispatched the whole array to the local office of the publication and awaited results. A few days later the editor, coming to Boston, sent for me. My application had been specially

75

remarked, and after making note thereon that I would accept forty dollars a week, he said that it would be considered. A silence of some days ensued, which I myself broke by writing directly to the head of the company. This brought a response from the publisher, who asked me to come and see him in Philadelphia. I did not get the forty dollars a week—then—but I did get the position.

CHAPTER FIVE

A TYPE EXPERT IN PHILADELPHIA

CHAPTER FIVE

A TYPE EXPERT IN PHILADELPHIA

 ARRIVED in Philadelphia early one Monday morning, enthusiastically happy over the prospect which lay before me. I remembered the inspiring rise of that other Boston printer who first trod these streets in the early morning, eating a roll as he came. With a purse better lined than his, I breakfasted at Green's, but as I struck into Arch Street opposite the office of my new employer, I paused by the iron grating of the quiet churchyard where Franklin lies, and with bared head paid my silent tribute to his memory.

The Philadelphia of 1892 seemed any-

79

thing but the "decaying place" he had
found it, and "The Ladies' Home Journal," though not the great publication it
is to-day, had already begun its extraordinary march towards success. Established
in 1883 by Mr. Cyrus H. K. Curtis, without capital, it was edited for the first six
years of its life by his wife under the name
of Mrs. Louisa Knapp. Some two years
before my coming, Mr. Edward W. Bok,
a young man who had served his literary
apprenticeship with Charles Scribner's
Sons, had been intrusted with its editorial
direction. Widely heralded as the young-
est and highest paid editor in America, he
had no easy task before him, but his ability
was as remarkable as his opportunity, and
the magazine sparkled with new life.
Many novel series of articles piqued the
public interest: "Unknown Wives of
Well-known Men," "Unknown Husbands
of Well-known Women," and most effect-

ive of all, a Famous Daughters number, to which the children of Thackeray, Dickens, and other literary celebrities contributed.

Meanwhile the "Journal's" typographical appearance remained unchanged until the publisher, Mr. Curtis, one day conceived the plan, new at that time, of issuing a periodical which should be artistic from cover to cover. This meant that he must not only use better illustrations, but replace all the black and heavy types, then used for advertising, with the lighter styles just coming into vogue. To carry out this revolution was my task, and to me, knowing little of advertising, it seemed to present no great difficulty. But my cheery optimism struck an immediate snag in the simple fact that advertisers prepared and electrotyped their own announcements, and having in many cases used the same advertisement for years,

81

had come to reverence its crude yet familiar features as the cause and mascot of their prosperity. Yet here we came with the impious proposal that if they wished to advertise with us, the sacred fetich must change and purify its face!

We had to make our own precedent in this matter. One newspaper, the "New York Herald," had laid down arbitrary rules forbidding display type altogether, and formed its larger letters by combinations of the capitals of usual reading size; but there was no instance of such action on the part of a magazine publisher, and our clients rebelled most vigorously against the innovation. Accustomed to deal with publishers who would accept any copy, they would frequently hold back an advertisement till the last moment in the hope that it would slip into our pages unrevised, but intuitively sure of my employer's backing, I tried

82

the drastic remedy of leaving these late-comers out. This, though effective in some cases, had its financial drawbacks, and I resorted to the gentle expedient of a registered letter to all advertisers, acquainting them with our rules of display. To insure the better printing of the magazine, I explained, all advertisements must be reset in our own type. We could use no electrotypes sent us, but if sufficient time were given, we ourselves would be glad to submit proofs for approval; otherwise advertising matter must undergo such modifications as would permit its insertion under our rules. Open war followed. Taking the offensive themselves, they flatly refused to pay for advertisements thus inserted. But they fought in an out-of-date cause. A valuable medium, steadily growing in favor, the "Journal" could not be ignored, and as its appearance improved, their desire to make use of it strengthened. Inevitably they came to our way of thinking, settled their unpaid bills, and continued with us on our own terms.

In this general housecleaning black cuts naturally had to go. This reform was, in its way, more difficult than the change of type, because it often necessitated a new engraving at our own expense; but in this work, too, the support of my chief was sure. It is often said of Mr. Curtis that once he has the right man in the right place he gives him full sway. Certainly I could not complain on this score. I was given sufficient rope to make or hang myself. Only once in all my typographical changes did I consult him. A full-page advertisement, the price of which was $3000 for the single issue, had put me in a quandary. Arriving just before we went to press, the proof bore the warning: "Will not accept any change in this

84

advertisement," yet its top line, "How to Feed the Baby," was displayed in as flagrant disregard of our new rules as big black type could make it. To leave out a full page now was a serious matter, for beyond the money loss loomed the necessity for alteration of the magazine's makeup. Hoping to get permission to reset the line in lighter type, or to "stipple" it, I set the long distance telephone humming, but it was a Boston client, and in the Massachusetts calendar that particular day stood consecrated to Bunker Hill. Hanging up the receiver, I decided to leave the decision to headquarters, and taking my way in some trepidation to Mr. Curtis, I showed him the proof. He gave it a brief glance.

"Well, what about it?"

"It doesn't come within our rules of display," I answered.

85

To my relief he did not ask me to define them.

"You're the doctor," he said tersely, and handed the proof back.

I felt that explanations were due, however, and pointed out that the page must either go in as it was, or be left out altogether and reading matter found to take its place. Its money value being what it was, I had hesitated to act without consulting him. At this he turned in his chair and delivered some axiomatic truths about weak-kneed publishers who went to the wall because they did not adhere to their rates, gave out inflated circulation statements, formulated policies and broke them, and committed other sins common at the time. But of the page in hand, never a word!

Our mail a few days afterwards contained a letter from the advertising manager who had sent me the omitted

86

advertisement. One paragraph ran : "As we have never been favored with a copy of your rules of display, would it not be well to send us either a framed or an un-framed impression of these impediments to business, to hang in our outer office for our own reference, and as an awful example to the many representatives of other publications who call upon us?" We retained this advertiser's business notwithstanding.

Out of this endeavor to make our pages attractive throughout grew a policy which, as far as I personally was concerned, came to wear the aspect of a crusade. I had been with the "Journal" but a short time when there came a six-time order for an advertisement of a certain sirup of hypophosphites, set in a black type which I saw must be changed materially. To its subject matter I gave no thought. Endorsed by physicians, it had the ear-

87

marks of a first-class advertisement, and as such had received Mr. Curtis' sanction. I knew little or nothing about patent medicines myself, for in my home they were never used, my father's only cure-alls being tincture of rhubarb and tincture of turpentine; but after this special remedy had paraded its claims before my eyes for several issues, I began to investigate proprietary medicine as a whole, and to perceive something of the vast range of fraud and quackery which lay behind its philanthropic mask. Choosing an opportune time, I suggested that it would be to our benefit to decline, not only this particular advertisement, but patent medicines of every kind. Mr. Curtis' assent was immediate and hearty. He said my predecessor had failed to use good judgment in this matter, that he personally had no desire to accept such advertising, and that he was glad I understood it. So began, modestly enough, a course of action which was to have consequences more far-reaching than I dreamed.

While these problems were, one after another, meeting solution, there simmered in my mind a thought which I hoped time might translate into something more substantial. It took its rise from a letter which our Boston agent addressed me perhaps a week after my service with the "Journal" began. There was nothing remarkable about the contents of this letter, but its envelope gave me the title "Advertising Manager." What did it mean? Inexperienced as I was in the details of the business with which I was grappling, I had few leisure moments, but whenever the chance came I would fish this envelope out of a drawer and recall a piece of advice given me years before: "Put your ambition high, and work up to it." For some time, however, I would always slip the envelope back again with the reflection that I had much to learn and must make good my present footing before I bothered my head with titles. The "department" at the outset consisted of myself and a desk, but my employer, hearing that I often worked far into the night, presently instructed me to hire a clerk to keep my records. This spare time gained, I began to study how to better myself. To improve the typography of the "Journal," to make it up in first-class shape, and to keep a record of the accounts were my ostensible duties, but in thinking over my experience as a salesman, I saw no reason why, if I could sell types and printing presses, I could not also dispose of advertising, and so prove myself of further value to the house.

I saw my chance in the "Journal's" back cover. Full-page advertisements were rare, even at this time of low prices, and the back-cover page usually held four announcements, though in dull seasons even eight would sometimes mar the space which I reasoned could be more artistically and more profitably devoted to one. My plan to utilize our cover in this manner was quickened by the fact that " The Youth's Companion," with half a million circulation, was beginning to insert full-page advertisements prepared and sold by Mr. Francis A. Wilson, then the most successful promoter of advertising of a truly national scope. It was a novelty for a publication to prepare advertisements for a customer, but as advertising agents had already suffered shocks at our hands, I could see no harm in administering a few more, and with the firm resolve to sell full pages to some of our clientele, I began to scan our order book for likely victims.

At that day advertisers would contract

for a definite period, with the privilege of increased space at the same price, thereby gaining an advantage over those less prudent, if the rate in the meantime advanced. Selecting my man, provisioned in this way, I spent several days analyzing his advertising, and then formulated a full-page announcement which, I believe, struck straight at the heart of his special needs. My complete plan included a handsome wood engraving at the top of the page, but wood engravings meant money. At this pass I went to Mr. Bok, who had often complimented me on my achievements, took him frankly into my confidence, found him a willing listener, and gained his consent to incur the necessary expense. But for that bit of encouragement from a fertile mind, ever open to ideas from others, my advertising career might perhaps have been nipped in the bud. As it was, it bore fruit almost as soon as planted. Long before this, of course, I had made my advertiser's acquaintance by letter, and I had now only to tell him that I meant shortly, on a trip to Boston, to stop off, meet him personally, and show him an advertisement I had prepared. I had chosen well my customer, a future friend, and the day I sold him my first full page remains one of the happiest memories of my business life.

My arrangement with the "Journal" stipulated for an increase of salary at the end of the third and sixth months, but inasmuch as at the close of the eighth month I had secured by personal solicitation nearly $6000 worth of advertising, I requested that beginning with October my pay be raised from forty to fifty dollars a week. In the formal reply the treasurer said, that while my services were fully appreciated, they deemed my application untimely and recommended that any further requests for an increase be deferred to the end of the

year. But this disappointment was soon
forgotten. For years, without any re-
quests whatsoever, my remuneration continued to grow, and on the announcement
of my forthcoming marriage another un-
expected increase in salary came my way.
Taught diplomacy by this, I went gingerly
about that other project which had its inspiration in the envelope still reposing out
of sight in my desk drawer.

There was a sound reason behind my
ambition to wear the title of the office I
filled in fact. Personality nowhere counts
more than in the advertising business, and
as my correspondence grew I saw the
need of emphasizing this factor. Feeling
sure, however, that any direct suggestion
on my part would come amiss, I arranged
a little *coup d'état*. Planning a letterhead for the exclusive use of the Advertising Department, I had my own name
placed in one corner in very small type.

94

The treasurer's name, on the contrary, bulked quite as large as a treasurer's should, and my modesty won his gratified approval. But there remained Mr. Curtis. Without his authority the engraved letterhead bearing my name was waste paper. Delaying its use, therefore, I watched my opportunity, and in the course of routine it came. Having a few days later to confer with him on an important matter, I submitted a letter on the subject which, as regards contents, could not fail to meet his approval. In heading it was open to doubt, for it was written on the new paper. The letter, true to my expectation, passed muster. The heading escaped comment, but not notice. The following day he, in turn, showed me a letter, wherein to my great satisfaction he referred to me as "my advertising manager."

Not long afterwards I ran across a

sailorman who, years before, had captained a relative's yacht in which I had enjoyed many outings in Boston Harbor. On his asking what I was doing, I rippled off: "I'm advertising manager of 'The Ladies' Home Journal,' Philadelphia."

"I don't know what that means," he said, his moon face wreathed in smiles, "but it sounds good."

CHAPTER SIX

ADVERTISING MANAGER OF
"THE LADIES' HOME JOURNAL"

CHAPTER SIX

Advertising Manager of
"The Ladies' Home Journal"

ANY account of my own activities as advertising manager of "The Ladies' Home Journal" should be prefaced with a word about the striking campaign for a larger circulation set on foot by Mr. Curtis before I entered his employ. No such project had been attempted since the days of Robert Bonner. The latter, so the story goes, took whole pages of space in the "New York Herald," and in small type duplicated, a thousand times or more, the single line: "Fanny Fern writes only for the 'New York Ledger.'" The cost was of course great, and his friends thought him mad; but when the pastor of his church, a man who never read an advertisement, called to show him the error of his ways, Mr. Bonner had a clear vision of his ultimate success. So it was with Cyrus Curtis. The publishing world prophesied bankruptcy, but he footed his extravagant bills with a stout faith. Aiming at a feminine clientele, one of his first and most telling moves was to follow the advice of his agents, N. W. Ayer & Son, and take large space in "The Delineator," which, with a circulation of half a million monthly even then, was spreading broadcast fashions to exploit its paper patterns. This counsel was disinterested, for the usual commission given advertising agents was denied, but it would have been cheap at any price. "The Delineator's" rates were low, and $6000 spent in announcements, cleverly prepared and exceptional in size and style, so beguiled the women of the country that Mr. Curtis, as sure as Bonner of his final victory, straightway decided to disburse $1000 a day for a year.

The full benefits, naturally, did not accrue at once, but the course of display so lavishly begun was all the time making for success, and work in plenty developed for the department of which I now became the responsible head. Continuing the plan of preparing announcements for advertisers I had used so successfully in selling my first full page, I designed others with such good results that Mr. Curtis hit upon the idea of establishing a " Service Bureau," and engaged Miss Jennie Frazee solely to write advertisements. A delightful little woman who wrote as she talked, she had won her spurs with the drygoods house of Barr Brothers, of St. Louis, where her work attracted Mr. Curtis by its originality.

Her advertisements were aimed at the average customer, not the literary critic, and if one caught her up for a lapse of grammar, she would reply, "Yes, but that's the way the majority of people would say it." Her coming necessitated the services of an artist, and we accordingly enlisted the aid of Miss Jessie Willcox Smith, now well known as an illustrator. Announcements written by Miss Frazee and illustrated by Miss Smith proved successful from the outset, and when advertisers, who usually took twenty-five or fifty lines, saw the work of these clever collaborators, they would double, triple, and even quadruple their space. Other artists were soon needed, and our bureau was further strengthened by the work of Miss Violet Oakley and Miss Elizabeth Shippen Green, who also have since achieved marked distinction in the world of art.

At this time I entered my first and only

prize contest. Allcock's Porous Plasters were my theme, and as they had alleviated the penalty of too long hours at my desk, I wrote in full sympathy with the subject. In one inspired evening I produced a series which brought me $150, the first prize.

Advertising was then placed mainly by advertising agents, and one of them, Mr. J. Walter Thompson, of New York, finding it impossible to obtain a special rate in the "Journal," not unusual for him in other publications, now proposed, in consideration of a five per cent discount, to pay for all advertising in advance, a check to accompany every order. As Mr. Curtis' expenditures were enormous, this suggestion from a man who placed an immense volume of advertising held advantages too great to neglect, and with the understanding that other agents should receive the same discount for such payments, this radical departure from custom was adopted. Soon

after my coming to the Advertising Department we issued a new rate card, and
announcing this plan, added that we should
deem advance payments proof of an advertiser's or agent's financial stability. The
rigor of this rule was later modified to
allow five days' grace from the date of the
bill; failure to settle within that time, the
postmark of the letter being admitted as
evidence, serving to deprive the tardy of
any discount whatever. To the manufac-
turers of dress goods and other feminine
wear the notion of paying for advertisements nearly a month in advance seemed
revolutionary in the extreme. They gave
their customers from three to six months'
time, and dated their bills ahead at that!
But the "Journal" was a powerful medium, five per cent was five per cent —
and they fell in line.

This scheme of payment made it necessary to forward copies of the magazine to

advertisers in advance of publication,
to the end that they might see their
announcements before ordering the next
insertion. For a number of years, therefore, our advertising clients would receive
a complete copy three weeks ahead of
the reading public. But one day there
appeared in a Philadelphia daily, ac-
credited to a Chicago newspaper, a poem
by Eugene Field, which a too zealous
exchange editor had cribbed from some
advertiser's advance copy of the forthcoming "Journal." The press of a push button
brought about an immediate consultation
with the justly indignant editor, and I
was asked, as soon as might be, to devise
some effective check upon thefts of this
nature. Half an hour later Mr. Bok's face
lit with surprise and pleasure as I laid
before him a "dummy" which solved
the problem. It contained the cover, the
advertisements, and the titles of the

articles, but of other matter not a stickful. In this form, the reading part blank, it went out thereafter, and so continues to this day.

Owing to definite agreements and other causes, several of the patent medicines to which I have already alluded for some time remained a thorn in my side, but hoping to be rid of them all by and by, I had to content myself with making full-page glorifications of Beecham's Pills, Scott's Emulsion, and Dr. William's Pink Pills for Pale People as inoffensive in type and copy as I could. Cuticura was especially difficult to whip into present-able shape, but I wrestled with it to such good purpose that a full-page advertise-ment of the soap ran monthly, yet with-out affront to the eye, for nearly a year. As Mr. Curtis' publicity campaign brought business from other sources, these prob-lems, and in fact the whole body of

106

objectionable advertising from which they sprang, gradually dropped out of sight. The very first medium in the publishing world which an advertiser put upon his list, we could afford to pick and choose and be as fastidious as we pleased.

Many fallacies were dispelled here, many theories tested. One interesting advertising fact we developed was woman's undoubted influence over man. A manufacturer of men's suspenders, for example, thought it a waste of money to advertise in a woman's magazine. We proved him wrong. Following up this idea, probably the first political announcement aimed at men through women now appeared in our publication. Paid for by the National Republican Committee, it devoted a page to an entertaining tale of a woman who went abroad thinking she could buy superior dress goods cheaper than at home. Samples of fabrics were illustrated and prices compared. High protection was then rampant, and the little tale reached the inevitable climax that the fair traveler returned to America without buying anything. The advertisement was headed "Where I Purchased After All."

Some numbers of a magazine, particularly those of April and November, always overflow with business, and as advertisers are prone to wait till the last moment, I put in practice another novel method. Two days before we closed one of these issues my assistant handed me a memorandum to the effect that if we received all the copy for which we had orders and promises, every inch of space would be filled. Needing all the time I could get to arrange this specially large amount of business, I accordingly wrote this telegram :

"Please do not send any more advertising for the April number, as the space is fully taken."

Showing this to Mr. Curtis, I told him that I meant to send copies of it to every one of the forty odd advertising agents of the country. Here, as always, lengthy explanations were needless. Handing the telegram back, he said: "Good idea. Send them." Half an hour later my assistant came with a sad face to tell me that she had made the mistake of counting a full-page advertisement twice. Telling her to be more careful in the future, I cheered her up with the assurance that the message would bring to us more than the four columns we lacked. And so it proved. Never does an advertiser long to use a publication so much as when he is barred out. These strategic telegrams of mine roused much favorable comment in the advertising world, but when similar messages left our office in the future, the space was actually taken.

While things fared so well in my department, the Western office, under the management of Mr. Thomas Balmer, was such an important factor that the advertising from the West often more than equaled the amount obtained in the East. To Mr. Balmer, more than any one man, is due the credit of lifting the advertising business to the high plane it now occupies. Bringing to his work a long experience gained in other walks of life, he suggested ideas which in some cases seemed Napoleonic, but which we know as standard policies to-day. Realizing that a truly scientific advertising must base itself on psychology, he set to work to analyze business failures, and conclusively proved, among other things, that the advertiser who buys small space pays dearest. Again, scrupulous of the ethics of his profession, he originated the contract plan between agent and publisher which makes it obligatory for the former to retain the publisher's full commission and give rebates to no one. These instances indicate the remarkable caliber of the man who, becoming the first Western representative of an Eastern publication, ever carried out the policies of his home office with unflinching loyalty and a firm hand.

During my connection with "The Ladies' Home Journal" I saw many business managers come and go, and as I wished to broaden my experience of publishing, I took it into my head that, when the next vacancy occurred, I would make a bid for it. Presently the chance came, and I told Mr. Curtis that I believed I could fill the place acceptably. He pointed out, as I felt sure he would, that neither in salary nor rank was the position as important as my own. Whereupon I brought to light my carefully devised plan of driving a double team, or, in other words, acting as business manager and advertising manager at the same time, with an assistant in each department. His rejoinder to this ended the interview. "It is not my policy," he said, "to put two departments in the hands of one man."

I should not have been myself, however, had I not made that attempt. The aspiration to get on which spurred me from office to office as a union printer still persisted, and undiscouraged by this rebuff, only bided its time. Casting my eye over the magazine field, I saw possibilities in the "Atlantic Monthly." Printed at Riverside Press, it was the first magazine of which I had any knowledge. A great publishing house was behind it, with a list of books by famous old-time authors as well as newer favorites. As a business proposition for the book end, the idea was sound if, as I planned, the magazine could be increased from its small circulation of less than twenty-five thousand copies up into the hundred thousands. To do this the "Atlantic" would have to be materially changed and illustrated. On one of my trips to Cambridge I pointed out to my old friend, Charles Walker, this striking opportunity, and he, speaking of it to the publishers, brought about an early interview. The delightful gentleman who has been for so many years the head of this old house was interested, but to change the magazine in any way — never! It was Boston.

As was generally the case wherever my lines were cast, my next difference of opinion with my employer hinged upon the question of salary. Indeed, with the exception of Mr. Curtis, I had never worked for anybody who raised my pay as often as I thought I deserved. I was not always right in so thinking, for when I became an employer myself, I learned that rapid promotion may handicap a young man's use-

fulness. Be this as it may, I had these
notions about my services, which, until I
came to Philadelphia, no one seemed to
appreciate at their full value. Here, for
five years, increases came regularly. Then
I was forgotten, or at least it seemed so,
for one day the looked-for raise failed to
appear. Selling personally large quanti-
ties of advertising space in addition to
many full pages, I believed my work
should be better paid and resolved that,
if I could not persuade my employers to
agree with me, I would again get out into
the world of opportunities. Nothing developing at the next meeting of the board
of directors, I frankly petitioned Mr.
Curtis for $5000 a year. My reasons
were two : I felt I was worth it, and I
needed the money. To the latter argument he dryly replied that whether I
needed the money or not was a personal
matter in which he had no interest. As

for the salary, he stated that so many heads of departments had requested more pay for their subordinates that the total amount involved had decided him to delay all increases for another year.

My disappointment must have been evident, for a few days later I was told that I might go abroad at the company's expense — a suggestion I had often advanced — and that in the fall the salary I asked would be mine. Supplied with ample funds and followed by a *bon voyage* telegram from the editor, I set out on my first transatlantic trip. The outing broadened my point of view and put me in the way of meeting many advertisers and advertising men whose acquaintance later proved valuable assets. I now first came to know the hospitable courtesies of Mr. Thomas J. Barratt, managing director of Pears' Soap, whose remarkable offices and beautiful home with its art collection, which

included Millais' "Bubbles" and Land-
seer's "Monarch of the Glen," I found
full of interest.

The fall saw me back at work and
my salary at the $5000 mark promised.
Those were piping times everywhere, and
the "Journal" rode on the crest of the
wave. Totaling a quarter of a million
dollars at my coming, the business of
my department now had a yearly volume
of twice that amount. It was the heyday
of advertising, and the salaries of advertising men were beginning to mount with
the profits. Repeatedly, I could have
gone to newspapers at a higher salary.

About this time " The Saturday Evening
Post," a story paper, was bought by Mr.
Curtis. Its assets consisted of its name
and the fact that it had been established
in 1728 by Benjamin Franklin. To me
this purchase naturally suggested an enlarged department, more work, and

116

probably an increased salary, but this vision of larger usefulness seemed remote. "The Post" could have no future without the miracle of a rebirth. This was, of course, before Mr. Curtis discovered in Mr. George Horace Lorimer a co-worker whose editorial ability well matched his own signal talent for exploitation.

By normal standards I should have been content. But I was not.

Systematized to the last detail, the Chicago and the New York offices practically independent, my department ran with the precision of a faultless machine. I had leisure now for reflection, and reflection told me an unwelcome truth. Lodged permanently among the odd scraps of philosophy by which I steered my course was a watchword given me by a well-disposed friend early in my business life. "Don't get into a rut, my boy," he warned. "If you find you are in one, pull yourself out quick." Was I not in a rut now? I had been with the "Journal" six years — a long time for me to work for one employer. If I were not to become, as I hoped, a vital part of this concern, would not continued service unfit me to do battle elsewhere? In the fiercely competitive business world I had watched new men come and old men go. A mere employee, I too, some day, my maximum usefulness past, might tread their melancholy way.

Speedily, and yet with deliberation, I set down my thoughts in a letter to the publisher, which I sent to a Boston friend for revision. This friend, an advertising agent well acquainted with Mr. Curtis, had acquired the art of "smooth" writing. My own style is to call a spade a spade, and not "an agricultural implement for removing the crust of the earth," but I realized the importance of this step and wanted the best advice possible. I received the advice, and my chief the letter. I said that I was satisfied with my position and my salary, but in contemplating the future, as a young man should, it seemed to me that "I should be placed where others of my class are: with such a stock interest, in addition to a fair living salary, that I could feel myself a part of the integral whole, all working for a common end." This, I suggested, could be arranged by giving me an option on $20,000 worth of the company's stock. Mr. Curtis' reply was not "smooth." "There is no such quantity of stock for sale," he stated, and as the flash in his dark eyes met mine, I read that my future was to him another "personal" matter in which he had no concern. I was as a spoke in a wheel, a part of his great machine, and I had failed to interest him beyond the day's work. I did not take umbrage at this, though to know it was worth while. Men, who are not slaves, make of their lives what they will. Before this brief interview ended, there flashed across my mental vision other positions which I had declined; other possibilities in the world yet untried. To my optimistic nature change still meant progress. To take one more roll, before the moss gathered, was my determination. And I saw another milestone near; another break in the life-line of my business career.

Within a month I resigned, having meanwhile secured a position as business manager for Frank A. Munsey. I asked no advice this time. Men of affairs, seeking counsel of their fellows, desire merely to have their plans approved. Munsey was considered impossible. Other men had gone to him and stayed but a few weeks. All advice would be against the experiment. Therefore I sought none.

Just before I left for New York my friends — rich, well-to-do, and poor — gave me a costly farewell dinner at the Bellevue Hotel. I had never figured so publicly as guest of honor, and touched by this tribute, I promised myself that I would some day show my appreciation. As the feast neared its close the chairman received and read this telegram:

"To be dined and wined upon entering a town is one thing. To be dined and wined by friends and business people after six years of citizenship is quite another thing. I wish I were with you to-night to join in personal felicitations to Mr. Thayer. — FRANK A. MUNSEY."

CHAPTER SEVEN

A Month and a Day with Munsey

CHAPTER SEVEN

A Month and a Day with Munsey

FRANK A. MUNSEY is a brilliant man — in more ways than one. A real genius seldom makes a success of a business undertaking, but a man who is a genius in spots can be successful in business. Munsey is a genius in spots. During the financial panic of 1907 his purchases of common steel were so large that he made millions of dollars on the rise in values, and those who followed his advice at that time likewise profited, as I have good reason to know. His career as a publisher is a most interesting tale. Braving New York with "a gripful of manuscripts and about forty dollars in cash"—to use his own words—he for years faced what seemed almost sure failure. Seeing plan after plan crumble, doing two men's work by day, writing his own serials at night, meeting changing business conditions with fresh ideas, and finally, $100,000 in debt, fighting a single-handed battle with a great distributing monopoly which tried to shut him from his public—such was the rise of the man who after a quarter of a century found himself owner of several daily newspapers and many monthly magazines.

It has been said by a rival that "Munsey is not a magazine publisher, but a magazine manufacturer." As it is a known fact that the Frank A. Munsey Company's annual profits exceed $1,000,000, it is clear that, as far as earnings go, he is the most successful "manufacturer" in the magazine world. Some men issue magazines at a loss; Munsey makes his to sell. It was not a manufacturing publisher who drew the above distinction.

My first day with Mr. Munsey stands out in my mind as distinctly as the one, when a boy, I was promoted to long pants. I was told that first morning to attempt no actual work, but to " breathe in the atmosphere of the place." This was a new line of work for me, but I did my best. My arrangement was for a year at a salary of $7500; our actual relationship lasted for a month and a day. The story is best told in two letters and a prophecy.

As a New Year's present, the following letter was handed to me at the close of day, December 31, 1897:

"New York, December 31, 1897.
"My dear Mr. Thayer, — This week which ends to-night completes your fourth week with us. I have been studying you

I suppose about as closely as I should expect you to study a new man in your department. If I were in your place and you in mine, I should be glad to have a frank statement from you of the impressions you had formed of me. Feeling this way myself, I naturally assume that you would like to know what impressions I have formed of you, and for this reason I write you this letter.

"In a word, you are not the strong man I expected you to be. You have shown nothing of the versatility I expected to find in you, nothing of the alertness of temperament I expected to find in you. You have brought no new ideas to the house, no new ideas to the advertising department. You have brought no business, either directly or indirectly, to the advertising department in the four weeks you have been here — not so much as a line. You have shown no extraordinary genius in your correspondence; you have written no advertising, have got up no advertising. And in your handling of the force you have not evidenced any remarkable executive ability or even first rate diplomacy.

"When you complained yesterday that I did not show sufficient confidence in you, I replied that you had done nothing yet to command my confidence. You answered that it was three months before you did anything at 'The Ladies' Home Journal' [*sic*]. Be this as it may, I submit to you that there is a very wide difference between the young man direct from a typefoundry, with absolutely no knowledge of the advertising business, and no pretence of knowledge of the advertising business, and on a nominal salary —between such a man and a giant in the business, a full-grown man, a fully equipped man, a great big salaried man.

From the one I should not expect much, from the other I have every right to expect a great deal.

"Such answers as these on this point show a lack on your part of a closely reasoning mind, and no man can appeal to me, can command my confidence in a managerial position unless he shows well-thought-out reasons for every act, every move he makes, every statement he makes. This is only one of the instances that lead me to believe that you are not a close reasoner. Moreover, your tendency towards red tape, your tendency to surround yourself with a halo of exaggerated importance, your petty jealousy when a man from the advertising department comes to me, or I send to him to come to me—all this is extremely distasteful to me, and will not go for a minute in this house.

"In the four weeks you have been
130

here you have hardly been out of your office. I expected, as a matter of course, that you would lose little time in putting yourself in touch with the advertising agents and with the army of advertising solicitors employed by these agents, to say nothing of bringing your personality to bear upon the leading advertisers of New York and New England. I made it quite plain to you a few days ago that the course you were pursuing did not appeal to me as the wisest one, and I think you announced to Mr. Ridgway that hereafter you would be in your office only a small portion of the time, or something to this effect. But in discussing the matter yesterday or the day before you told me that there were so many of our solicitors in town that it was not wise for you to go down and recover the ground. In a word, if it is not wise for you to do this, and if it is not wise for you to establish a

131

personality with all these men as the representative head of the department, then it is not wise for me to keep you as the representative head of the department.

"Now I will tell you, my dear Mr. Thayer, just where the great big mistake has been, and there is no question in my mind but that you have made a mistake and that I have made a mistake. You have overestimated your capacity to do for us and underestimated our capacity to do for ourselves. This is the mistake you have made. The mistake I made was engaging you on the great big reputation you had, the glowing statements of your friends, and the showing you made for yourself in the several conversations you had with me.

"Here is what Mr. Barber said to me in Boston one day last fall. 'There is a possibility, Mr. Munsey, that you can get a great genius in the advertising business.'

132

'Yes,' I said, 'who is he?' 'Who is he?'
Mr. Barber replied with a smile.   'Why,
there is but one man in the whole country.' After a good deal of fencing, and
the promise of strict secrecy on my part,
I learned that that one man was Mr.
Thayer, of 'The Ladies' Home Journal,' and Mr. Barber assured me that it
was Mr. Thayer who had brought the
advertising department of 'The Ladies'
Home Journal' up to its matchless standard — stood for the department, made
the department, was the department.
And Mr. Barber added that, with 'The
Puritan' on my hands in addition to my
other publications, if I could have the
assistance of Mr. Thayer, could have Mr.
Thayer at the head of my advertising
department, I need have no further
thought of it, and that Mr. Thayer would
make such a showing as we never could
hope to have without him.

"Well, all this impressed me tremendously; it would have impressed most men
tremendously. Then, too, there was Mr.
Clark's statement to the effect that you
were a wonderful business man, a man
of rare energy, an indefatigable worker,
etc., etc., etc.

"These are the causes that led to my
mistake, and I think I stated accurately the
causes that led to the mistake on your part.
You may not be ready to grant even yet
that your coming here was a mistake, but
from my point of view there is absolutely
no doubt about its being a mistake at the
salary at which you came. No man, I do
not care who he is or what his line of work
is, can afford for a minute to allow himself
to accept a salary bigger than he is himself.
The minute he does this that minute he is
at a serious disadvantage.

"It is possible you might be worth this
much, or at all events a good handsome

salary, to a house that knows nothing of the advertising business itself, to a house having a moderate knowledge of the publishing business, but here it is different. Your mind has not covered a wider range of thought than the combined minds operating this business, and your experience has been less rather than greater than that of the combined forces operating this business. This being the fact, you have brought nothing to the business, no knowledge we did not already have, and as to your individual capacity, candor compels me to say that we have with us half a dozen men whose average salary is one-third of yours, all of whom are men who can make themselves of greater value to me than I believe it possible for you to be.

"This is a straightforward, unbiased, and as kindly a statement as I can make of my impression of you at the end of the four weeks with us. I regret exceedingly that

135

I cannot make you a report that would be full of glowing praise, but it cannot be done.

"With this statement before you you will not be misled. You can bring your reasoning powers to bear upon the problem, and together with me, help to figure out the wisest way we can both get out of the mistake we have made. I regret the mistake vastly more on your account than I do on my own, and it is my purpose to treat you in the most generous possible way — to do whatever I can for you to help you in making other connections or to help you in starting a business of your own — something, anything that will be to your best interest and to my least disadvantage. I can better afford the loss than you can, and I want to stand back of you to the greatest degree possible in all rational considera- tion. Between us we ought to be able to devise some plan that would let you out

136

without injury to your reputation. The sooner some move of this sort is made the more I can afford to do for you and the better it will be for you in every way. Feeling as I do, you see how unwise it would be for you to attempt to go on seriously with the work. On the other hand, it would be very unwise for you to seem not to go on with the work as usual until some definite plan is fixed upon between us. There is no reason why this thing cannot be handled gracefully, cleverly, and satisfactorily to both you and myself. It will depend very largely upon your disposition in the matter, upon whether you accept my view in the case gracefully and reasonably, or whether you oppose it in a way to annoy me.

" Let me repeat that above all else, above all personal consideration, I want to help you to the greatest possible reasonable

137

degree in getting out of the mistake we have jointly made.

"Let me say one word more. If you prefer to stay here throughout the year, and for which I agreed to pay you a salary of $7500, you may stay. I made a year's agreement with you at this salary, and it shall stand if you wish it to, but to my mind it would be a most unwise thing for you to do.

"Very truly yours,

(Signed)   "FRANK A. MUNSEY."

A Sunday and a holiday came with this letter. Perhaps you can imagine the feelings of a man who, only a few weeks before in a position considered to be the most prominent in its line in the country, now, in his change for betterment, found himself, at an inopportune time and under adverse conditions, cast out into the "cold, gray world."

138

Notwithstanding this letter, I was not crushed. The last paragraph, in which Mr. Munsey put into writing his agreement with me, up to that time only verbal, was an earnest of the honesty and fairness of the man.

As an uninterrupted conversation with Mr. Munsey was quite impossible, I wrote him the following letter:

"January 3, 1898.

"My dear Mr. Munsey, — I have your letter and I admire the frank way in which you have put the matter. I have naturally been studying you very closely, but this letter tells me more than a dozen interrupted interviews. You are a wonder to me, and the more I see of you the more I wonder and marvel at the great success you have made and are making. My study has developed the fact that you reason closely, but sometimes — often —

your quickness of perception is colored — changed — altered entirely by your emotional instincts. I realize that you are slow to put confidence in anyone, but I say most emphatically right here at the start that you engaged me for a definite purpose, and I should have your confidence from the beginning, and that confidence should not grow less until I make serious mistakes or exercised bad judgment. I came to you on the record I have made, and when you say I lack all or any one of the business qualities that go to make up a progressive business man, you accuse my former employers of lacking business acumen and sense and imply that my business friends — men with whom I have come into contact and know me for the work I have done, know me for the business I have taken from them personally — are blind, ignorant imbeciles.

" If you were manager of a railroad and

engaged an engineer you would tell him:
'There's the train; there's your assistant;
there's your schedule, go by it. I want
you to run that train and I'll look to you
for its safe arrival at its destination." If,
however, before the train started you told
the fireman that he could use just two
shovels full of coal an hour and gave the
conductor and trainhands to understand
that you didn't want the passengers
hurried, etc., you could not expect results,
until such time that you decided that was
not the way to run a train.

"I have been in New York four weeks.
I have been put in a cage and you have
walked around and looked at me and said
to yourself, 'He's not doing anything.'
I knew you were studying me, but baffled
at every turn in attempts to do anything,
I could do nothing but think of what was
needed to be done and of the results that
would come from such action.

"Taking up the advertising end of the business: I do not overestimate my capacity to do for you in this line, for it is run in the most expensive and un-businesslike manner, and the results are far from what they should be. Advertisements are inserted without any order; conditional orders are accepted and the conditions not complied with; advertisements are charged at the wrong price and charged to irresponsible agents, etc., etc. —the general idea everywhere being to get through the day and take no thought of the morrow.

"My judgment tells me that we would have just as much and more business if the agents and their solicitors and the advertisers were not seen so often. The principal reason why advertisers use your publications is because they have value. This is the thing that should be impressed upon advertisers by letter, by circular, by an occasional personal call. Where friendship secures one order, merit, rate, and circulation bring twenty. Too much personal solicitation is annoying to the advertiser and agent. This personal plea of asking advertisers and agents to send you advertisements to put money in your pocket is a false theory to work upon — every prominent advertiser and agent will tell you this.

"I believe that both Mr. Barber and Mr. Clark gave you their honest opinion. Mr. Barber said in your words, 'If Mr. Thayer was at the head of your advertising department you would need to have no thought of it.' He meant this, and I am certain that he is right in the matter, for I managed an advertising department with an income of nearly a half million dollars, and there is no reason to think for one moment that when I left that department

143

I also left my brain, my sense, and my judgment in Philadelphia.

"You didn't tell all that Mr. Clark said. When I told Mr. Clark, after my resignation, that I had heard from you that he had said good things of me, he told me that you wouldn't tell me all he said. This was to the effect that I would do for you if I was given a chance — if you would let me do something. He also affirmed that I couldn't do anything, for you wouldn't let me. I went on to tell him that I didn't believe anything of the kind. I had been with two large concerns whose owners wanted to run everything, but I found that they were very willing to drop part of their labor on my shoulders. And when they discovered that I was a man who could assume responsibility, do things satisfactorily and bring results, they were glad to have it so, for it made their mind free for other and more important things.

"With you now, whether you believe it or not, you are showing the strain of overwork. You will feel this more as time goes on, and you will have to drop it. What better thing could you do right now than to throw on me the advertising end of the business? You doubt my ability? If you have such doubts it is because your overworked brain leads you to doubt everyone. Your great business needs me much more than I thought it did. There is lots of work. Much time is wasted by lack of a little system, expensive salaries paid without proportionate results.

"The salary of $7500 that you are paying me is meager, compared with the results that I could show at the end of the year. How much money did you lose last year in unpaid accounts? Do you know? You are aware of the fact that good judgment in this particular alone is worth at

145

least twenty-five per cent of the amount you lost last year.

''I should be false to my own honor, my loyalty to you, if at this time I should give up thoughts of making your success much greater.   In the years to come I expect to see your great publishing house the first in the land, its fame world-wide.   I anticipate a success that will far surpass that of Sir George Newnes.   At that time I will be glad to stand by your side as one of the faithful lieutenants who has done his part to bring this about.

''Look around at the men who have overworked their brain — the result is always the same.   You may have more power than any of them, and I believe that you have.   There is a limit, however, to all power, all endurance.   You will admit that Sir George Newnes has made a wonderful success.   Take him for an example: how has he done it?   By looking after

146

every department of his business? No, indeed. His advertising manager told me in London that when Sir George wanted to see him he gave him twenty-four hours' notice; when he wanted to see Sir George he gave a week's notice and the appointment was made. This could be called 'red tape'; it is carrying things too far.

"I know that I can manage the advertising end of your business, perform all the functions of the business management to your entire satisfaction, but not, however, unless you believe in me, in my worth, in my ability, in my judgment.

"It is a necessity for you to have loyal lieutenants who understand business methods. Your business has grown so fast that you did not have time to educate young men. You have engaged me as a man who knows, without further education or training. There is lots to learn in your great big business. I am yet a young man;

147

I'm pliable and can change ways to meet the situation. You need the benefit of my education, my training, and my year's service will prove this to be true, and the 'bright and brilliant' men who think I have made a mistake in coming to you will hold a different opinion of the matter — will have a different opinion of the great personality whom I now hail 'Chief.'

"Faithfully,

(Signed)   "JOHN ADAMS THAYER."

But my reply did not change the state of affairs. Mr. Munsey rejoined that he had given thirty days' long, deep, earnest thought to the problem before he wrote me. "Were you in fact a man of all the strength that your reputation gave you, with *my* estimate of your ability you would be so seriously handicapped that it would be impossible now for you to work out the problem here for which you came."

148

A few days after the passing of the letters I sat in Mr. Munsey's office, which was then on the eleventh story of the Constable Building, looking down on Fifth Avenue. It was raining. The flickering lights below, the hurrying cabs and people all told of the end of another business day. It was the end, too, of my term with Munsey, a milestone on the road of my career. After a long-continued conversation we had reached a settlement. I was to give my resignation and receive a check for $2500, and that I might go abroad, an order for one page of space in ''Munsey's Magazine,'' worth $500, and good for the advertisement of any steamship line. This was in addition to the salary I had drawn weekly. Financially, the settlement was satisfactory, but I was keenly disappointed to lose the year's service and its consequent experience. Mr. Munsey believes himself to be a close reasoner, and this, probably, was the cause of his insisting, in defence of his arbitrary action: "Thayer, I say again that I will do anything I can to help you. I hope you believe that I have treated you fairly. But I must reaffirm to you that you are not the strong man your friends represented you to be." I started to interrupt him, but he continued, "Five years from now will prove it, whether you believe it at this time or not."

If you were a scratch golf player, and someone to belittle your knowledge of the game said that you and Colonel Bogey were eighteen holes apart, would you not feel indignant?

I was indignant. I jumped to my feet, raised the forefinger of my right hand, and looked him squarely in the face. Then, with the emphasis an energetic advertising man often uses to clinch an important deal, I told him that he had given me no opportunity to do anything for him; that he was

150

absolutely mistaken in his estimate of me. I closed the interview by assuring him, and the words came deliberately, that it would not take five years to prove him wrong. Handicapped though I might be by his action in forcing me out without a chance to show my ability, I would do it in less time.

CHAPTER EIGHT

A Year with a Newspaper

CHAPTER EIGHT

A Year with a Newspaper

BUT I did not go abroad. Indeed, I still have among my assets the order for a page of space in "Munsey's Magazine"; I toured New York's publishing houses instead, looking for another position. It was not a cheering experience. For gossip, no village sewing circle can surpass the advertising fraternity of the American metropolis. A story will illustrate its possibilities. Two well-known advertising men agreed to say to the first magazine solicitor they met, "Have you heard that Mixon is to make a change?" Upon a reply in the negative, they were to add, "Well, if you have n't

heard of it, don't say anything about it."
Each, it was understood, was to speak to
but one person. Now Mixon held an
enviable position. He had been for years
the advertising manager of one of the big
magazines, enjoyed a very handsome salary,
and entertained no thought whatever of
leaving so snug a berth. Suddenly he
found his peace troubled. Forty-eight
hours after the jokers dropped their seed
on Broadway, it bore fruit in Chicago in
the breast of a man who wanted to suc-
ceed Mixon and wired to bespeak his
influence. This was but a foretaste. The
next few days showered him with con-
gratulations, and his bewildered firm with
inquiries and applications for the position
he was to vacate. There was nothing
vague or halfway about these statements.
They had a ring of downright fact which
his employers thought demanded explana-
tion. In the upshot, the victim even felt it

necessary to announce in " Printer's Ink," an advertising journal, that the rumors were absolutely without foundation.

Such conditions are more amusing to hear about than to confront, but facing the gossip myself, I took a Mark Tapley pride in being jolly under depressing circumstances. I could put up well enough with the sorry-for-you tone of voice and the I-could-have-told-you-so friend, but it was less easy to learn that some people thought the great woman's magazine had made me, and that without it as a prop I was down and out. I had known men to leave good positions only to find themselves worse off. But I would not admit that such was my case. In a dark moment, however, the thought did come to me that Mr. Munsey might be right in his estimate, and it startled me to such an extent that I put my head in my hands, as I had done many times before when the occasion was less serious, and fought the issue squarely to a finish. Reviewing the long struggle I had made, I could come to but one conclusion: I had been dumped out on my life's journey by an accident. I had misjudged not myself, but my vehicle.

While I cast about for exactly the best opening, I deemed it best to "get out of the wet," as the saying goes, and my umbrella took a form I had little anticipated. My calls on the publishers and advertising men had been fruitless. My Munsey salary, which was known, seemed to stand as a bar, and no offers were forthcoming. In the vast quantity of information I collected in these rounds, however, I came across the serviceable hint that "The Boston Journal," a daily newspaper, needed an advertising manager. I cannot say I was tempted. Indeed, when I recalled my first newspaper experience,

158

it took courage to face the prospect at all. While I was in Philadelphia, as I have mentioned, I had several opportunities to become advertising manager for dailies, but I did not look favorably on such work. That they appeared daily was one great drawback. Another, more vital, was the fact that they then thought nothing of running all sorts of patent medicine and objectionable advertising.

But a newspaper was better than stagnation, so off went a typewritten letter to Stephen O'Meara, who was the "Journal's" publisher. In applying for the position I pointed out that there were some things, as yet untried by dailies, which could be pushed to success with a strong conservative paper such as his own. The advertisements could be set in a manner new to Boston; they could be written more effectively; they could be illustrated artistically — all with the aim of attracting the large drygoods

159

houses which, unlike Wanamaker's and
the great firms of other cities, neglected to
make adequate use of publicity. This letter
appealed to Mr. O'Meara, as did my reply
when, at a later conference, he broached
the question of pay. I said frankly that I
did not wish a big salary—just enough to
live on would do; but what I did want was
a percentage of the increased business which
I would bring to his paper. This suited
him precisely, and I once more took up
life in my old home.

Naturally, I brought a fresh pair of eyes
to bear upon my birthplace. Boston, as
one of her noted sons has said, is unlike
other great American cities. ''Some of
her institutions, through antiquity or association, have acquired a positive sanctity.
Pedigree is important. The average in-
habitant spends much of his time watching
the grandson of his neighbor's father to see
the old man's characteristics crop out in

him. The boy's failures will be remembered against his own offspring fifty years hence. It is a city of long memories and traditions." I now met this dead weight of the past at every turn. With "The Ladies' Home Journal" I had dealt with large advertisers, and I expected to reach a similar clientele here. But the pillars of Boston commerce were another race of beings altogether. As regards advertising, the great majority of drygoods merchants still dwelt in the Middle Ages. They put in a new elevator occasionally; they now and then enlarged their stores; but, prosperous by Boston standards, they saw no reason why they should change their outworn methods of advertising. Entrenched behind their Chinese Wall of indifference, I found them as difficult to get at as the residents of Bar Harbor, who, in my one experience as a book agent, would neither see me nor the volume I had to sell.

Finally, I drove an entering wedge with the house of Shepard, Norwell & Company. Mr. Edward E. Cole, the junior partner, a man of keen business caliber and old-school amiability, became interested in my ideas, and told me he had planned a similar innovation some time before with Mr. Lorin F. Deland, whose advertisements, though simple, were remarkably effective. Mr. Cole ordered a half-page advertisement to appear weekly for six months. I was not only to advise and suggest, but write and illustrate the items in any manner I saw fit. In pursuance of this plan I would even take hats and garments of various sorts from the store for an artist to sketch before I wrote my own copy. With this beginning one would think, as I thought, that other firms would prove easily accessible, but such was not the case. Often the heads of houses refused to see me at all, and the one chance I had of talking to perhaps the most prominent of them was obtained by standing guard till he issued from his private office. I approached him, stopped when he stopped, walked on when he walked, and so, following him round his great establishment as he made a journey to a distant department, I put my argument as best I could. He would hardly listen and kept referring me to his advertising manager, a man without power, on whom I had already wasted many hours. Knowing that his prejudice against my paper had its source in an offensive news item, I pointed out that years had elapsed since it appeared; that the "Journal" was under entirely new management and, a stronger medium in every way, would bring him sure returns for his advertising if he would only try it. It was no use. This was Boston of the long memory. He could not, even for profit, forgive the paper which long ago exploited the

163

news that his son had married without
his consent.

But I had been in similar predicaments
and had no doubt of the outcome. I remembered an amended proverb quoted
by a former employer: "All things come
round to him who will but wait"—if he
hustles while he waits. My task was to
build up such a medium as would compel
people to advertise. I had already abol-
ished the black, inartistic type used by
other Boston dailies for headings and advertisements, and the new faces wrought
a great improvement in our typographical
appearance. But I realized that something
more unusual than this must be done to
acquaint advertisers with the fact that the
"Journal" had taken on a new lease of
life and energy. It has fallen to me more
than once in my experience to hit on ideas
in advance of the times, and the proposition it now occured to me to employ was

one which later became very popular, and under the name of Sunday Supplement, is a feature of many newspapers in America. I suggested to Mr. O'Meara that he reduce the "Sunday Journal" to half its size, and using a larger type and better paper, make it in effect a weekly magazine, with the news of the world thrown in for good measure. He began to smile, as I continued, and took from a drawer of his desk a showing of half the Sunday issue in the form I advocated. He was pleased that he had anticipated my suggestion by a year or more, and as this made my own way easier, I was no less glad. Few men of ideas get anywhere in this world unless they harness power to their originality. The valuable idea is the idea which — in the expressive slang of the day — delivers the goods.

So it was that, barring the news section, the Sunday paper was halved in size and doubled in quantity of pages. The type and paper did not conform to my plan, but we had taken the step, which was the main thing. Following up the campaign, I urged Mr. O'Meara to publish daily the figures of our growing circulation. To this he demurred, saying that we would suffer by comparison with the grossly overstated statement of the "Boston Herald." But just here seemed to me our opportunity. His knowledge of the "Herald's" real standing being exact, I persuaded him to offer to give $1000 or so to some hospital if our rival could prove to a selected committee of advertisers that its circulation came within fifty thousand of its printed claims. This appealed to him, and we were soon in the thick of a circulation war with the battery all on our side. The breastworks of the enemy were soon leveled by the pungent editorials for which Stephen O'Meara was noted, and not long afterward, with a change of management, the colors fell too, and the circulation figures were withdrawn.

This controversy and the change in size proved most effective. Circulation increased and orders for advertising so multiplied that one Sunday, in addition to many columns of smaller advertisements, I marshaled eleven full-page announcements of local houses. As the receipts naturally showed a healthy growth of several thousand dollars each week, I deemed the time ripe to ask my chief to put our scheme through in its entirety. But Boston conservatism once more blocked the march of progress. He was gratified with my work, but stronger than his ambition to see the "Journal" use better paper, larger type, and modern illustrations, was his wish to repay his friends some of the money they had advanced him to secure control of the property. My argument that they were wealthy, had no need of the money, and

167

would beyond doubt approve of the change was of no avail. He agreed in theory, but balked at practice.

In two other things I met disappointment. I wanted to see advertisements take their proper place at the bottom of the page, instead of alongside reading matter at the top in the clumsy fashion to which Boston still clung; and I longed for authority to turn all objectionable advertisements from the door. But these policies involved decreased receipts for an indefinite period, and decreased receipts, though they meant an up-to-date publication, were unpopular in the counting room. I made the best of the situation, hoping presently to see a loophole for further reform, but the future, instead of accommodating me, produced the Spanish War. This event, while not materially affecting Boston, made a vast difference in the plans of general advertisers, and with

the cancellation of orders of this class, I
found that my successful local work merely
stopped the gap of a deficit. After the
battle of Santiago, the general advertising
returned, and this, coupled with my local
business, plainly indicated that if I could
renew my contract on the same terms, my
second year would net me a handsome
income. When the matter came up for
discussion, however, I was again made to
realize that I dwelt in the city of sanctified
traditions. I was told that for the year to
come I must be limited to $7500, which
was "a good salary for Boston." This
final example of conservatism so disgusted
me that I resigned on the spot.

A half hour in my own office, with my
head in my hands, altered my point of
view. I again went upstairs and with a
smiling countenance said I had thought
the matter over and concluded that, after
months of hard work, day and night, I

was tired out. If he approved, I would withdraw my resignation and take a vacation. Mr. O'Meara readily assented, as I felt sure he would, and I went to Cuba.

Vacations have properly slight relevance to this story of a business career, but as on this particular outing I for once saw history in the making, it perhaps deserves a digression. Arriving in Havana on the afternoon of December 31, 1898, the day before Spain surrendered the island, I presented to Major-General Ludlow a letter of introduction from the son of one of his close friends, and asked for a pass which would enable Mrs. Thayer and myself to see the next day's ceremonies at the palace. He referred me to his Adjutant-General, who was with him at the time, and the pass was presently forthcoming. I was unaware that President McKinley, out of consideration for Spain, had cabled instructions that the ceremonies should not

be public, only the militia and two Press
representatives to be witnesses; and in the
same ignorance I set out the following day
for the palace. American troops guarded
the building, but the general's pass took
us by without delay in the wake of a group
of gentlemen in evening dress. Following
their lead, we entered, by mistake, a side
entrance of the palace, and to our surprise
found ourselves in the private apartments
of Governor-General Castellanos. Knowing no Spanish, I could only extend my
pass to his secretary, but the card worked
its immediate magic, and amidst bows from
the assembled suite, which made our way
seem like a royal progress, we were ushered
to the throne room. This great chamber
we found tenanted only by ourselves, but
as we glanced from its immense windows
into the plaza we saw on a near building
a group of Americans, among whom we
identified the wives of generals, senators,

171

and other notables who chanced at that time to be in Cuba. Believing now that a mistake had certainly been made, I displayed my pass to a gentleman in a wonderful uniform and was assured in musical Spanish, of which I understood not a syllable, supplemented by gestures as plain as English print, that our location for the ceremonies was absolutely perfect. So it proved. I looked at my watch. It was five minutes to twelve. At that instant rose the solemn strains of the Spanish anthem. As it ceased there was a moment's silence. Then up through the casements came the Star Spangled Banner, and the procession, which had formed below, wound its way through the great portal and up into the room where we were. Major-General Brooke, and the officers under his command, their dress uniforms and yellow sashes a bright note of color, entered first; then came the

172

swarthy Cuban leaders, their uniforms less splendid, but their dignity beyond question; and last of all, General Castellanos and his staff. The scene was too painful to prolong. A moment of formalities and it was over, and the defeated said farewell. It was an ordeal for a man of Castellanos' temperament. Tears came to his eyes. "I have been in many battles," he faltered, "many trying situations, but never in a position like this." Then, as we watched, the little handful of Spanish troops, headed only by fife and drum, set their faces towards Spain. The drama which began with Columbus was finished.

Returning to my desk, I took up work again with my old-time energy, but having by now gaged the possibilities of Boston, I worked with an eye open for another position elsewhere. It was not long in appearing. Just at this time Mr. George W. Wilder obtained control of the

173

Butterick Publishing Company, a million-dollar concern in New York, manufacturing paper dress patterns and publishing a monthly periodical called "The Delineator." This great enterprise, of which his father had been the brains, had through mismanagement fallen into a bad way, but by hard work Mr. Wilder and his brothers finally purchased the stock interest of Ebenezer Butterick and secured the direction of its destinies. Casting about for an advertising man, he consulted the advertising manager of the American Tobacco Company, who, at Mr. Wilder's suggestion, wrote to ask if I would entertain an offer. He was, he remarked, looking not for the most brilliant man in the business, but an honest one; a requirement that shed a certain light on the task with which that man would have to cope. A few days afterwards I went to New York, and a brief interview settled my engagement.   Our plans we threshed out a week later at Mr. Wilder's country home, Cheshire Place, in the New Hampshire hills, where I pointed out to him the great possibilities I saw in "The Delineator," and showed him the first real rate-card which that sadly bungled periodical was to possess.

CHAPTER NINE

BLEACHING A BLACK SHEEP

CHAPTER NINE

Bleaching a Black Sheep

EORGE WARREN WILDER, the real head of the Butterick Company, has a sense of humor. Returning from lunch with him and some of the staff one day soon after I became his advertising manager, I was escorted to a pair of Fairbanks' scales in the shipping department. With solemn mien my new chief indicated that my weight was to be taken, and after prolonged adjustments of the various digits, it was as gravely announced that I tipped the beam at one hundred and eighty-eight pounds. Whereupon leaving the other witnesses of this rite behind, he took my arm, led me by devious ways to an obscure, seldom-used office, and carefully closing the door, turned the key.

"You have been here long enough," he said, his face all seriousness, "to know that the advertising department of 'The Delineator' has been grossly mismanaged. We have had no fixed rate. For years advertisers and advertising agents have had no confidence in us. We lack character. Now I believe you will remedy this, for I am told that you are the very man in the advertising world who can do it best and do it quickest. It means much to me, for I have great plans for enlarging this business. You will have a very hard job to bleach this black sheep of ours, but it will be worth while." Then, his blue eyes lighting with amusement, he added with a smile: "Forget your weight taken to-day. You're going to lose a lot of it."

I found the sheep not only as black as he had stated, but unsound in body in other ways for which, as an advertising man, I had scarcely expected to prescribe. During my days in the New Hampshire hills, I had blue-printed the possibilities of the future so strongly on Mr. Wilder's mind that that ever-active organ demanded prompt and tangible results, but these involved more than increased advertising receipts. Better printing, better illustrations, improved typography, attractive front-cover pages, and logically, a larger circulation, were all imperative. In all these matters, outside my province, I assisted materially, and the selection of the circulation manager and his assistant, the art director, and the foreman of the composing room where our advertisements were set, also devolved upon me in the course of my service. It was natural for Mr. Wilder to advise with me in these affairs, for his own knowledge of the publishing business was meager, but my

181

all-round zeal brought down on me the displeasure of the heads of other departments, who could not make out why an advertising man should suggest and push to completion ideas which did not pertain to his specialty. They did not know that my knowledge of publishing included every branch of the business, and I had no occasion to explain. Of the paper pattern department—familiar to the women of countless households—I had no knowledge. Nor did I seek it. I believed that if I concentrated my abilities on the problems of publication, Mr. Wilder's hopes would be the sooner realized.

Meanwhile, I had my particular share of the black sheep to look after. Of my association of nearly four years with the Butterick Company, the first twelve months were at once the most difficult and the most interesting. My arrangement ran that, if I increased the advertising receipts by $50,000 during the first year, my salary should be $10,000, but, this incentive aside, I realized that the plans for enlarging the business made a larger income from this special source of high importance. With a circulation of nearly half a million monthly, "The Delineator" had been issued primarily as a catalogue of its pattern industry, and its advertising receipts, which at the time of my coming averaged $136,000 a year, were merely incidental.

It is very difficult to establish a fixed price for advertising in a publication which has never had one, but this was what I now had to do. The advertising agents of America who handled the business which was worth while had lost all confidence in "The Delineator," but they knew me, and when I announced that the rate was now two dollars to all comers they showed their faith to a man. Perhaps I should say, except one man. There was a Doubting

Thomas who, holding the magazine's past in sore remembrance, could not believe his ears, and requested me to put the amazing new doctrine in black and white. He had lost many orders in the past because of the dickering and cutting which had prevailed, and wanted a letter guaranteeing him a rebate if he could prove, after sending us business, that any other advertiser or agent had secured a lower price. I not only gave him the guarantee he asked, but offered him access to our books, files, and correspondence should he harbor suspicion in the future. I had never met the man or dealt with him in any way, but my letter convinced him and he became a constant client thereafter.

Once made, I kept the rate as rigid as the laws of the Medes and the Persians, disappoint whom it might. This sometimes had humorous consequences. Perhaps a month after I took hold of the

184

department I received a letter from Mr. Charles E. Raymond, the Chicago manager of the advertising agency of the J. Walter Thompson Company, enclosing an order for one of his customers at the old rate. He explained that, on account of absence from the city, he had neglected to send it before or write me concerning it; and as Mr. Raymond was then, as he is still, a dependable man in his field, I knew he wrote the truth. It was important that no exceptions be made, however, and I accordingly replied that I knew he was acting in good faith, and that under ordinary circumstances his order would be accepted, but the advertising department of " The Delineator " had such a dubious past that I would do nothing to stir even a breath of suspicion in the future. I closed with a reference to the man who lived so upright a life that he leaned backwards, saying that, while I did not want to appear to play

185

that role, conditions were such that I must decline his order. Mr. Raymond's laconic answer ran: "Dear Sir,—You are leaning backwards."

A curious paradox of this question is the fact that, although it is suicidal for a publisher to have more than one price for advertising of the same kind, it is yet possible for a publication to contain in the same issue announcements of three advertisers all charged at a different rate. A rise in circulation naturally involves a better rate, but a notice of an intended increase is customary, and up to a specific date the publisher will take orders to run a year at the ruling price. Sometimes a publisher is forced to take such action oftener than yearly, with a corresponding shortening of the time allowance, and so it fell out that during my connection with "The Ladies' Home Journal," "The Delineator," and later with "Everybody's

Magazine," there would be advertisements at different rates in a single issue, though the periodicals were on an absolutely one-price basis to all.

The end of the first year found the rate firmly established, but the receipts of my department, owing to my war on the objectionable advertisement of which I shall speak in detail later, fell $7000 short of the expected increase of $50,000. But I was highly pleased with our showing notwithstanding, for "The Delineator" was unmistakably on the upward march. Moreover, my work gained me the maximum salary after all. The undesirable advertising I had refused was taken into account, for, as one of the firm pointed out, there was no reason why I should be punished for working for the best interests of the business.

During all this time I had in the back of my head the intention to get my old-

187

time friend and co-worker of " The Ladies' Home Journal" to assist me. I needed the strongest possible man in the West, and that man, beyond a shadow of a doubt, was Thomas Balmer. But how should I persuade Mr. Wilder to add to my staff an assistant who would demand a salary equal to my own? The right opportunity seldom fails to come to one who can curb his impatience and bide his time. I recognized the "psychological moment," which novelists are so fond of mentioning, as I sat, fishing-rod in hand, on the bank of a pond at Cheshire Place.

"I'm going to get a stronger man in the West very soon," I dropped as casually as if it were a mere question of bait.

"Are you?" said my host. "Who is he?"

"Thomas Balmer. The strongest advertising man in the world."

"What!" smiled Mr. Wilder. "I thought you were it."

I assured him that Mr. Balmer had no equal as a result getter, and was undoubtedly what I had just said, — the greatest man in the business. With this opening I proceeded to outline his progress as Western manager of "The Ladies' Home Journal," and the innovations for which the advertising world in general was his debtor. The question of cost followed, and I said that while I knew he had declined many big-salaried offers, I believed I could get him to come to us for my own salary if he might have the same increase when he proved himself worth it. Whereupon Mr. Wilder interrupted: "Let's go over to that other pond. There's more fish there."

With the requisite authority I left New Hampshire the next morning, happy in the thought that I was sure of a stanch

189

ally in the special reform I had so close at heart. Even more serious to me in the bleaching process than the rate was the question of quality. As much as the company needed greater receipts and as I wanted to earn my maximum salary, I could at no time tolerate the thought of any compromise with my arch-enemy, the objectionable advertisement. I longed to drive it, not only from our own magazines, but, if I could, from the printed page everywhere. More than any other professional ambition, I wanted to see American advertising clean.

CHAPTER TEN

The Fight for Clean Advertising

CHAPTER TEN

The Fight for Clean Advertising

WHEN in the regeneration of "The Delineator's" advertising department, I faced the question of quality, I lost no time debating a policy. The only course I could pursue was the one to which I had so far consistently adhered: all patent medicine, objectionable and doubtful matter must be declined. But where draw the line? Fraudulent advertising is objectionable always, but objectionable advertising is not always fraudulent. There are grades in advertising matter as in conduct. Black and white are easily distinguished; it is with the grays that doubt comes.

It happened that one of these neutral cases arose soon after my coming, and I saw in it a chance for an object lesson more forcible than a Niagara of verbal argument. There turned up one day an order for a hair restorer, an advertisement which had found "The Delineator" a friendly medium for years. I decided to decline this order, but I wanted the company to know what I was doing; the official I picked out to consult was bald. As I put before him the large advertisement of the hair restorer, with its "Before" and "After" cuts of a man as ill-thatched as himself, I told him that the order amounted to $3000; that we had space for it; that it had run for many years past. I added that to me, however, it seemed a grave error to accept it unless it could do the things it promised.

"Do you believe in such things?" I asked.

"I!" he exclaimed. "Do you think that if there *was* a remedy, I'd have stayed bald for thirty years?"

In carrying out this policy, I had a most invaluable assistant in Mr. Balmer, who, with his high ideals, was naturally in sympathy with the idea. There was nothing halfway about our reform. It struck clear to the root of the evil. Many advertisers promised impossible values for trivial amounts, and it was not long before we announced that not only patent medicines and objectionable advertisements would be declined, but all which were extravagantly phrased. Thus an assertion that a lady's suit worth seventy-five dollars would be sent on receipt of twenty-five dollars in cash would be considered "extravagantly phrased" and the order declined, unless personal examination proved its truth. It is difficult to explain to the layman the detail with which every announcement

195

was censored. The word "cure" had to be stricken from every advertisement before it appeared in our columns. If a well-known make of vaseline was said to "cure" sunburn, we obtained the advertiser's consent to change the word to "relieve," or declined his money. In our printed communications to clients, as well as in the magazine itself, we enlarged upon what we were doing in this line, and made a bid solely for high-grade advertising. It came in good volume. So much so, in fact, that the close of our second year saw our total income from this source nearly $100,000 more than the year before.

But, as I have intimated, my crusade in this cause embraced a wider field than the columns of "The Delineator." I wanted to see this much needed purge universal. Nearly all the general magazines inserted advertisements of liquors, patent medicines, and other matter as questionable, and with the exception of the "Saturday Evening Post," published by Cyrus Curtis, the weeklies were also transgressors, the religious organs in some cases out-Heroding their secular contemporaries in guilt. The chief sinners of all were the great daily newspapers, many of which carried advertisements grossly fraudulent. I was characterized as a drastic reformer in my efforts to suppress some of this shameless trading on the sick and feeble-minded, and I daresay I deserved both the title and the epithet. Certainly, wherever I saw an offending head I hit it. My great opportunity came when I was asked to speak on any topic I chose before the Sphinx Club, an association of men devoted to various advertising interests. I delivered this address at the Waldorf-Astoria, October 8, 1902. My subject, illustrated by stereopticon slides, was

197

"Should a Publisher Accept Fraudulent and Objectionable Advertising?"

The daily newspapers furnished me with sufficient ammunition. Of the numerous humbugs they had helped foist upon the public I chose three conspicuous examples for comment: the "divine healer," Francis Truth; the so-called Lucky Box; and "Five-hundred-and-twenty-per-cent" Miller. The exploits of these charlatans are doubtless graven deep in the minds of their victims, but the general memory is a thing of wax, and it will do no harm briefly to recapitulate these outrageous swindles at which so many newspapers of America connived.

It is the press of New England which should bear the odium of Francis Truth's shameless success. This quack, schooled to unusual cunning among fakirs of the most dangerous type, easily found complaisant publishers to print his advertise-

198

ments, headlines and all, in the guise of news. Thanks to their trumpeting of his miraculous "cures," he established himself luxuriously in one of Boston's best sections and surrounded himself with scores of clerks who, with series of manifolded letters, "treated" the stricken and deluded thousands who could not flock directly to his door. To those who did come he showed a trophy room decorated with discarded canes, crutches, and braces. Among these convincing relics were also displayed the charred ends of many expensive cigars, for even the smoking habit came within the range of his divine activities. When the crash came, the office boy testified that these stumps had been smoked by the Healer himself after his exhausting labors for ailing humanity. But there were profits before the crash; ten months of profits, which accumulated at the astounding figure of $30,000 a week. Then

Francis Truth was placed under arrest. The publishers escaped.

Intellectual Boston, the haven of all cranks and ''isms,'' was also the friendly nursery of that monumental fake, Parker's ''Three Star Ring Lucky Box.'' This talisman, which cost less than a cent to manufacture and sold for ninety-nine, was made of wood and contained a suspended brass ring bearing three stars. The first advertisement announced that ''Boston was mystified.'' Trust Boston! It furthermore stated that hundreds had been made happy. Its heading was similar to that of a regular news story, and as news it undoubtedly passed with careless thousands. As the superstitious paid in their money and the swindle thrived, two-column announcements detailed the wonders it had worked. A woman lost her valuable watch; ninety-nine cents invested in a lucky box recovered it. A ship went down in fifteen fathoms of water; the sole survivor carried a lucky box. The happy possessor of another lifted the mortgage on his home — lifted it with the box. A Wall Street operator wanted a tip in a panic, a poor man wanted a job, a girl wanted to go to the Paris Exposition, a spinster wanted a husband — the lucky box brought them all their heart's desire. The lame threw away their crutches, the drunkard forsook his cups, nothing was impossible — in the advertisements! The crowning stroke of knavery was the injunction: "Successful people with health and wealth are requested not to send for any more boxes, as Mr. Parker prefers to deliver the remaining lot to those who are in greater need of this world's goods." Over seventy-five thousand of these boxes were sold, and when the postal authorities intervened twenty thousand letters still awaited delivery. The newspaper publishers of the Modern Athens, who ran this advertising, shared in the loot at the rate of $3.50 per inch.

W. F. Miller spread a still wider net. He began his financial career with a ten dollar bill loaned him by two friends. He ended it — after handling millions — in State's prison. Through the newspapers of New York, Philadelphia, Boston, and other cities he held out the glittering bait of ten per cent a week on an investment of twenty dollars. And he paid it — for a while. The timid pioneers who sent him their little capital found themselves drawing the astounding interest of 520 per cent, and every man-jack of them became, on a five per cent basis, a willing agent to coax others to send their savings to this wizard with the Midas touch. The advertisements continued, the money poured in. One week saw $70,000 withdrawn from Boston and Philadelphia savings banks to swell the flood which at high tide reached a mark not far from $3,000,000. Miller's press agent styled him a Napoleon of Finance. His scheme was certainly Napoleonic in its audacity. Nothing could be more simple. He paid the dividends out of the principal.

Advertising, and advertising alone, made Miller and Parker and Truth possible. Unabetted by the press, they would never have risen from the obscure ranks of the thimble riggers and the adepts at three card monte. And it is not the publishers who need the money who print such advertising; it is not offered to them. It is the paper of good standing, large circulation, and high advertising rates which gets the business and, open-eyed, becomes party to the fraud.

A bill, introduced recently in the Massachusetts Legislature, to prohibit the publication of certain paid matter in newspapers unless marked as an advertisement will be a corrective of many similar frauds.

Like others who attempt to remedy existing evils, I found myself in advance of the times. Nothing showed this more plainly than the difficulties I now met in trying to form a society for the suppression of fraudulent and objectionable advertising. Prominent men, identified with advertising, when asked to serve on the board of directors, regretted that they had not sufficient time. Others declined for the reason that they knew there were other men better able to cope with the situation. I vigorously advocated the formation of this society, engaged a secretary, and personally met the contingent expenses, but disappointed at the lack of interest shown, and finding it required too much of the time which I felt belonged to my employer, I reluctantly put the idea aside.

But the fight itself I did not abandon.

If I could not raise a regiment, I could at least do my part as an independent sharp-shooter. I accordingly stood rigidly by my creed in practice, and by letter and word of mouth did what I could to win over the publishers of other periodicals. This private campaign had one striking result. Among the letters I sent out was one to "Collier's Weekly." It was of the "Constant Reader" brand, which some-times has an influence with a publisher. It ran: "I see 'Collier's' every week and I find in it patent medicine and other ad-vertisements which 'The Ladies' Home Journal' and 'The Delineator' do not insert. Why do you accept such adver-tising? I am sure you do not need the money." A Philadelphia man fathered the communication, and the response, duly forwarded to me, was cheering. "Upon receipt of your letter," it read, "I called our advertising staff together, and we have decided, as soon as certain contracts are completed, to discontinue the insertion of such advertising." The letter was signed by Robert Collier, the brilliant son of the founder of this great house. Occupied as editor, this advertising phase had not been seriously considered by him. He needed but this word of mine to set him thinking. Filled with crusading zeal himself, Mr. Collier not only drove every doubtful advertisement from the pages of his famous weekly, but enlisting the trained intelligence of Mr. Samuel Hopkins Adams, printed the series of articles entitled "The Great American Fraud." These, combined with the vigorous attack made by "The Ladies' Home Journal," dealt patent medicine advertising the severest blow it ever received.

CHAPTER ELEVEN
MY MASTER STROKE IN ADVERTISING

CHAPTER ELEVEN

My Master Stroke in Advertising

HE Cinderella-like transformation of "The Delineator" gave me many knots to untie, and I count my handling of one of them the master stroke of my advertising career. It was not — as might be imagined — a contract for advertising space footing up into many thousands of dollars. Contracts of from six to twelve pages of space were not unusual. This, on the contrary, was the cancellation of an order, and its story — with its sidelight on the business methods of two kindred yet widely dissimilar nations — is not uninteresting. About five years before my engagement,

the Butterick Company entered into a contract with the Pears' Soap Company, of London, for back-cover advertising in "The Delineator" and a pattern catalogue or two, this space to be paid for quarterly on the basis of about six shillings per thousand circulation, the latter to be guaranteed under oath. Two years before my coming, the contract had been renewed for three years, with an option for still three more at the same price. Anyone can understand that with a circulation of five hundred thousand at six shillings per thousand the amount of money thus received for the back cover would be about $750. But here was a virtually new "Delineator," a well-printed and well-made publication, with page space twice the size of the ordinary magazine, and therefore qualified to ask twice the amount which the ordinary magazine of equal circulation could demand.

Upon learning of this contract with its ill-advised mortgage on the future, I took the matter up with the officers of the company, and a letter was dispatched to the London offices to see what could be done. Nothing was accomplished, however, for the London representative was not an advertising man, and when he broached the question, it was put in such a way that Mr. Barratt, the managing director of the company, declined to cancel any part of the order. Realizing how detrimental it would be to our interests to have such a long-time contract on our books, I arranged to sail for the other side. I had met Mr. Barratt previously, as mentioned in an earlier chapter, and knowing that there was really only one way of doing business in London, I decided to play the game strictly according to English rules. My first call on Mr. Barratt, therefore, was at a time when I knew he would not be in his office. I left a card with the name of my hotel, the exclusive Carlton, which I had decided to patronize because I remembered it had a place in Mr. Barratt's affections. Two days later I received a letter from his secretary asking me to call the next day at five o'clock. I suppose my call extended over an hour. We talked of London, of English art, English cathedrals, English weather — of course — but of the purpose of my visit not a word. Just as I was about to go, I casually mentioned that before leaving for Paris I should like to take up a business matter with him, and asked for an appointment. He as casually regretted that as he was leaving in about a week on a fishing trip he feared he could make no appointment. Finally, however, he so far sacrificed his sacred routine as to ask me to come in the next day. I was prompt and brief. First telling him of my work with "The Delineator," and of the

212

great strides that had already been made, I added that I found myself handicapped in my progress because I could not give an American advertiser any of the back-cover pages.

"What do you want me to do?" he asked.

I thereupon explained that since Mr. Wilder's son had secured control of the company he had enlarged its scope materially by the purchase of a competing company, which likewise published a magazine for women. Would he not be willing to give up six pages of "The Delineator" and use pages in the other publication instead?

"Will this assist you personally?" he asked.

"Yes," I said.

"Then I'll do it."

I cabled my office that evening, and a

few days later in Paris word came that
the first page vacated by Pears had been
sold to another advertiser for $1200.
But there still remained the ill-starred
option. Waiting till the existing contract
had nearly run its term, I brought up
the question of its renewal in a letter
to Mr. Barratt, in which I took pains
to state that I had looked up the amount
of money he had paid us for advertising, and was surprised to learn that
it amounted to over $100,000. I rea-
soned, of course, that when his conservative British eye fell upon this good
round sum he would feel constrained to
reduce his advertising in our mediums.
And I was right. He gave up his option,
discontinued for a time, and when Pears'
advertising again appeared, the regular
price was paid. By reason of increased
circulation and improvement in the magazine, the back-cover page of "The De-

lineator" brought $2400 within two years thereafter.

In the campaign to lift "The De-lineator's" circulation from the five hundred thousand we had to the million we obtained, we ourselves became extensive advertisers. Daily newspapers and other magazines were our chief mediums, of course, but for a time we also used the billboards to familiarize the public with a catch phrase I had devised. I tried more than a year to hit upon something suitable, but nothing came to me till one day I read an article on the psychology of advertising, by Professor Walter Dill Scott, who afterwards embodied his investigations in his two books, "The Theory of Advertising" and "The Psychology of Advertising," in which he made it plain that the direct injunction "Cut this coupon out and mail it to-day" would draw more replies than the less emphatic "Use this coupon."

Acting on this hint, I had reproduced the line in my handwriting, "Just Get 'The Delineator,'" and waited to see if the women of the country would obey. They did. To my personal knowledge the phrase even tantalized men into buying copies to satisfy their curiosity. One hundred thousand dollars were spent to popularize this phrase.

Early in the first year of my service, Mr. Wilder began carrying out his plans for the enlargement of the business. One day he said bluntly: "Have you ten thousand dollars?" "No," I replied, my thoughts skipping to the Boston savings bank where I had tucked away three thousand of Mr. Munsey's money. "Not all of it, but I can get the balance."

The conversation ended as abruptly as it had begun, but it had its sequel later in the announcement that I could buy a hundred shares of stock in the Butterick

Publishing Company, Ltd., for $100 a share if I could raise the money within a week. I had had one modest experience in finance in Philadelphia, where I borrowed money to buy a small block of "Ladies' Home Journal" stock, which I closed out on leaving the city; but this was a larger affair altogether. I had friends — and friends, but as I canvassed the $7000 variety I racked my brain making a list of those who, having the sum, might loan it. Eventually, by the process of elimination, I got down to five names. I went to the wealthiest man first. He lived in Boston, but had a summer home on the coast, and my acquaintance with him was such that I went to the latter, and, as he was away, waited for his return. He arrived late, but promptly invited me to dinner. As we took our coffee afterwards on the broad veranda overlooking the ocean, I made known the purpose of my visit. He

217

listened carefully, and telling me that I was probably paying twice over what the stock was worth, advised me against the investment. As he had related his own early struggles for success, first as a clerk in a drug house, and later as a manufacturer, I was much impressed. I knew that he was even more than a millionaire, and that $7000 was a small amount for him to loan me if he believed in the proposition as much as I knew he believed in me.

So reasoning I went back to New York. Conservative Boston had taken two days of the precious seven. However, there were five left, one of which was Sunday. Two Philadelphia friends were next on the list, and working late, I took the midnight train to the Quaker City. Philadelphia may be quieter than Boston, but it is less conservative. The first man I called upon heard me out with interest, told me that no man ever made money until he got

218

into honest debt, and promptly said, that
as I could probably get a loan from a bank
of sixty per cent on the stock, he would
endorse my notes. I was elated, thanked
him heartily, and departed. I thought it
wise, however, to call on my other listed
friend, and after telling him my story,
mentioned the offer which I had just received, and asked his advice. He volun-
teered to loan me the remaining thousand
dollars upon my note, but thought perhaps
he could let me have the entire amount in
cash, I to send him the stock as security.
He would advise me the next day. I thus
obtained the stock in the parent company,
and by the absorption of other companies
at different times later, my ten thousand
dollars doubled and tripled in value. But
that is another story, and of its kind most
interesting. When a captain of finance
like George Warren Wilder transforms a
company with a million dollars into three,

six, and then twelve million dollars of capital, he achieves what the great financier Morgan did in a larger way with United States Steel. And the end is not yet. The profit which came to me by the purchase of this stock was put to a good use, as I shall soon relate. Had I followed my Boston friend's advice, this story would never have been written. This was my last borrowing experience, for I went to banks thereafter—the only really legitimate place for loans.

Three years and a half went by. The concern which, as someone has picturesquely put it, began with a capital of "a ream of paper, a pair of scissors, and a good idea" continued its steady march towards the great financial success I have outlined. The share my own department played is most succinctly told in figures. The $137,000 received in advertising by the Butterick Company the year previous to my coming had grown, in the final year of my service, to over $600,000. It exceeds a million to-day.

One day, in the president's office, I saw the architect's drawing of a massive stone edifice, fourteen stories high, to be built for and devoted solely to the business of the Butterick Company. Facetiously, the treasurer remarked: "Look at your new building!" As I looked I thought: "Many a true word is spoken in jest." As treasurer, he well knew that my department made it possible.

But the new building never housed me. Mr. Thomas Balmer, my successor, occupied the sumptuous offices of the advertising director, for before the structure was roofed, I perceived a long-awaited opening to become a publisher myself. I had resigned many times before, but on this occasion I took my employer with me. As I said at the outset, Mr. Wilder

221

has a sense of humor. To all of our advertisers and advertising agents he sent a printed postal card on which my own name was blazoned in type which broke all rules of display. It read: "Wanted— A successor to John Adams Thayer."

CHAPTER TWELVE

PUBLISHING "EVERYBODY'S"

CHAPTER TWELVE

URING these many years of hard work to upbuild other people's publications I naturally had at the back of my head the idea of one day becoming a publisher on my own account, but my special knowledge of the field had taught me that it usually meant a long fight to put a publication on its feet.

The story of McClure's struggle had come to me from his own lips. I was a Philadelphian when he started his magazine, but we met from time to time, and he one day outlined his life. Boyhood, his college days at Oberlin, where his later partners, Brady and Phillips, were his

225

classmates; his varied experiences with Albert A. Pope, of bicycle fame, with the Century Company, with his own syndicate, and finally, with "McClure's Magazine" —all were passed in review, and I remember his adding that he had reached the enviable position at last where he did not care whether he made fifteen or a hundred thousand dollars a year. Change and rest were what he wanted now.

And there was Munsey. I could not forget his eleven heart-breaking years, his severe toil by day, his still more exhausting drudgery by candlelight when, as he himself has said, he made "a complete switch from red-hot actualities to the world of fancy," and by sheer force of will produced serial stories for his magazines at the rate of six thousand words a week.

Both these men gambled with their health and nervous energy; and as I realized the risks they had run, because

of their ignorance of the game, I resolved
to bide my time until I was assured of
two things: capital, or financial backing,
large enough to lift the venture over the
rough and stubbly spots always found in
the critical first year, and an associate as
familiar with the manufacturing branch as
I was with the advertising and business
end. But, the novice may ask, what about
the editor? The prosaic answer is, that
with a few notable exceptions, editors do
not make magazines financially successful.
It is far more difficult to secure a capable
advertising manager, and he will demand,
and probably receive, twice the editor's
salary.

Cognizant of these facts, I felt that I had
reached another significant milestone when
Mr. Erman J. Ridgway advanced the idea
of purchasing "Everybody's Magazine."
During my brief term as Mr. Munsey's
business manager, Mr. Ridgway and I

served a common employer, but as he was located in New London at the printing plant, we did not come into personal contact. After my return to New York, however, we occasionally met, and I received various letters from him, which I showed to Mr. Wilder in the hope that we could find a place for him as superintendent of the mechanical department. We were both convinced that in certain lines he had ability of a very high order, but the emergency not arising, nothing ever came of these talks, and, till we joined forces, our actual acquaintance was slight. In some of our casual meetings, however, he had mentioned his ambition to publish a magazine and his many futile attempts to interest moneyed men in such an enterprise, and it fell out, therefore, that when he brought his latest project to me, I saw in him the ally for whom I had been waiting.

I was eager for the experiment. After nearly twelve years as an advertising man I found my work monotonous. Aside from a steadily increasing salary, which had then reached probably the top-notch of the time, I had lost sense of progression and craved a new outlet for my energy. I found it promptly now. Monotony and stagnation were unknown in the days which followed. There was first the question of finance. To invest all my savings in a publishing venture was not my intention at the start. Ridgway, who was younger than I, had no money, so in talking over plans for the purchase we decided that we would take a third partner and let him finance our work, we to draw small salaries until we put the magazine on a paying basis. The thought of coming down from $1000 a month to $5000 per year had no disturbing influence upon me. When the matter was broached to Mr. Wilder, whom

I selected to be the "angel," a phase of business acumen appeared which I had not anticipated. It was simply this: I had the money covering one-third of the purchase price of the magazine—therefore I should back the venture; Ridgway, having no capital, could not do likewise, but an insurance policy would be taken out, covering his life, the premiums to be taken care of by the company until we had paid the purchase price of the magazine out of our profits and were out of debt. My optimism was such that I needed no time to consider this serious aspect of the transaction. I assented at once.

Definite negotiations were then begun by Mr. Wilder, whose experience in dealing with big men and big figures made it easy for him to put the matter in such a light that an offer of one-fourth less than the asking price of $100,000 was accepted. Fifteen monthly notes for $5000 each were

duly signed, endorsed, and delivered to
Mr. Robert C. Ogden, then the New York
partner of John Wanamaker, and the
magazine was ours. To be sure, the notes
had yet to be met, but as the payment of
the first lay six months in the rosy future,
we glowed with the self-satisfaction of the
improvident man who, settling his debts
in similar fashion, said, "I'm glad that's
paid and off my mind." Mr. Ogden's
final words showed that he shared our
confidence, and read to-day, have a ring
of prophecy. "Boys," he said in parting,
"I know you will make a big success.
That is the principal reason why I entertained your offer in preference to others
even larger. I want to see the magazine
win out handsomely, and as I am retiring
from active business, I shall watch its
growth with great interest. I believe it
is now on such a basis that I can com-
pare it to a peach tree, well-planted and

nurtured, with ripe fruit that needs only plucking."

We had our own notions about cultivating our peach tree, however, and in our talks with our readers, which we made a special feature, we stated just what kind of a magazine we proposed to give them. As we followed word with deed the news promptly got abroad that "Everybody's" was different from the common run. A paragraph, which appeared in a well-known weekly, bears witness to the impression we made, and in its way voices our ideal. It ran:

" 'Everybody's Magazine' begins to be something more than an entertaining ten cents worth of fiction and articles. An identity has been developed—a sturdy and aggressive identity all its own and full of interest and promise. Thus far the magazine has prided itself on the timeliness of its features and the healthy virility of its fiction. Now it has found itself entered on its own mission, headed out on its particular crusade. The keynote of this individuality is the article by Alfred Henry Lewis, 'The Madness of Much Money.' It is safe to say that it will be generally read and appreciated all over the country. Throughout this number the magazine shows a purpose to depart from the baleful worship of Mammon and its possessors, which characterizes so much of the writings in current periodicals."

When I entered their field, many publishers offered me frank sympathy, but as I am no pessimist I gave more weight to the cheerier welcome of Mr. William W. Ellsworth. "I congratulate you," he said. "You will get a lot of fun out of it." As the secretary of the Century Company, I felt that he, if anybody, ought to know, but I understood better the special brand of amusement he had in mind after he had told me a story of Theodore Roosevelt. Meeting the latter in Union Square one piping midsummer afternoon during his stirring term as Police Commissioner, Mr. Ellsworth expressed his surprise that he was not then enjoying himself at Oyster Bay, to which Mr. Roosevelt characteristically replied: "Do you think I could get more real fun anywhere than I am having right now in New York?" So it was with us. We worked hard, but the work was as absorbing as a game.

The objectionable advertisement loomed in the forefront of our problems, this time a more insidious enemy, because, like the Greeks, it came bearing gifts. In common with other general magazines, "Everybody's" at the time of our purchase was running patent medicine and other advertisements at variance with the

234

high standard I had set for myself. The
test came over an order for a number
of pages of a headache powder, which
reached us a few days after we assumed
control. Just at this juncture the advertising agent, who some years before had
edited my "smooth" letter to Cyrus
Curtis, dropped in to see me, and handing him the order, I asked his opinion.
I expected him to confirm my own conviction that, a publisher now myself, I
could do no less than practice the doctrine
I had so energetically preached. To my
surprise he disagreed.

"Other magazines are beginning to decline these things," he said. "Take the
money they turn away. Wait till you
have many pages of advertising. Then
you can afford to be more particular."

I thanked him for his advice, but the
headache "cure" went back. The next
day I joyously announced to my associate

that business was looking up; I had even declined several pages. Asked for particulars, I told of the temptation I had put away. He stared his surprise.

"But isn't that good business?" he demanded. "'Munsey' and other magazines take it."

"'Munsey' and the others can afford to take it," I answered. "If we can't make a success of 'Everybody's Magazine' without running the stuff I have declined for so many years, then we'll make a failure of it, and I shall lose my money and you—your time."

From that moment we were in hearty accord in this policy. The next day I sent broadcast an elaborate announcement of our policy. In this circular I told of our appeal to the agent, of our belief in his friendship, of our regard for his opinion. We felt, however, that in this instance he was wrong—hence the announcement.

236

We had use for the money, but in this reform we were leaders, not followers.

We now began advertising in the daily papers, but of our many advertisements, the first, though small, is best remembered. As our initial number was for June, we increased the output only ten thousand copies, for magazine sales are less as summer comes. A week after publication, the entire edition being sold, my professional eye saw an opportunity to advertise, and on the train to my office I formulated an advertisement headed "Our First Mistake." Reading the announcement to my co-worker, I asked his opinion. The day was a sultry one, and we were both fagged with the work on our first issue. Without hesitation he said, "Oh, I don't know. I guess not."

"All right," said I, and the advertisement in a dozen pieces went into the basket.

I had much to do and knew we would get along without its aid. No one little thing could stop our success. But on returning from lunch, Mr. Ridgway said he had been thinking it over, and that he did not know but it would be a good plan to advertise as I suggested, and thereupon mentioned a point of which I had not thought. So we sat opposite each other at our big flat desk, and I waited for him to write the advertisement. This done, he tossed it over.

"What do you say?"

I read it.

"Oh, I don't know. I guess not," I replied, and back I tossed it.

He thereupon tore the paper up and threw it into the basket.

The humor of our action struck us in an instant, and we looked into each other's eyes and laughed. I then suggested that he get his draft, I mine, and that jointly we prepare one which would suit. So we stuck together the torn fragments. The advertisement was sent to the leading newspapers of the country and was a great success. Our assistant editor, a most intelligent woman, told me that she read it without realizing it was our own till the very end.

With the editorial work of the magazine I did not concern myself. Mr. Ridgway directed this department with the aid of able editors, both men and women. I did, however, reserve the right to pass finally upon the contents before it went to press. Occasionally a picture or an article was cut out on my suggestion and others substituted. I had a hand, too, in "With Everybody's Publishers," which at the beginning was a strong feature of the magazine. The department "Under a Spreading Chestnut Tree" was also one in which I became interested. In fact, I recall that I paid twenty-five dollars to the man who suggested this heading and some stories which came with it. The stories were returned. The heading should have gone back also, for I found out later that this also was a "chestnut," having been used in a New York paper for many months.

I was always eager to get the type-written copy of "Frenzied Finance" before it went through the editorial department. Thereby hangs a tale. In one of Mr. Lawson's chapters he referred to a "meeting of the Board of Directors of the United States Steel Corporation, wherein Mr. Henry H. Rogers, having made his invariable plea for quick action, was interrupted by the president of the corporation, who blurted out: 'Mr. Rogers will vote on this question after we have talked on it.' In a voice that those who heard it say sounded like a rattlesnake's hiss in a refrigerator, Mr. Rogers replied: 'All meetings where I sit as a director vote first and talk after I am gone.'" Rereading this, after it had been put in type, I found that our editors had changed the species of the snake. Demanding a reason, I was informed that neither did snakes inhabit refrigerators nor rattlesnakes hiss, but that on conferring together in the absence of the editor-in-chief, they had decided to let the refrigerator remain, but to make it a black snake, which really did hiss. I instructed these sticklers for exact biology to restore the sentence to its original pungent form. A few days afterwards Mr. Ridgway, who was in the West, also noticed the alteration and telegraphed me: "Please have editorial department change black snake to rattlesnake as originally sent."

The man who turns the pages of his magazine in slippered ease seldom realizes the labor involved in its preparation. He appreciates that authors have written, artists plied brush and pencil, and editors racked their brains to provide these novelties which instruct or beguile his evening hour, but of the enormous mass of detail — the important little things — which lies beyond, he knows nothing. Who, for example, imagines that the weather enters into the magazine publisher's calculations? Yet it is one of the factors which must be considered when the monthly question, " How many copies shall we print?" presents itself. An April number issued during the last days of March will sag dismally if the usual bad days are passed before it reaches the news-stands. In fact, I should say that a too lamb-like exit of March would make a difference of twenty thousand in the sales of an edition of half a million copies. The caprices of climate aside, it is never an easy matter to gage the size of an edition save in the case of a gradual increase or a gradual decline of circulation.

Or take the cover design. Who considers with what effort it may have been evolved? In our early days we had much assistance from Ralph Tilton, son of Theodore Tilton, in handling this troublesome detail. It was he who proposed that we have autochromatic plates made from actual designs, photographed down to the proper size. While our first cover was not particularly artistic — it represented two hearts cut on a birch tree — it was yet different from all other magazine covers, and caused comment by reason of its sentiment and novelty. He formulated many other ideas for us, suggesting them often in less time than it takes me to tell of it. After "Frenzied Finance" began, the endless problems which came up in regard to business, advertising, and

243

editorial, crowded us so closely that we all, including the art director — who was very capable in his line — had difficulty in finding new designs, but in such emergencies Ralph Tilton never failed us. Once, when we were in desperate straits, I telephoned him to meet me at the Café Martin for luncheon. An idea was at once forthcoming. "You say your Lawson article treats of stock market operations. To me that suggests bulls and lambs. Why not go to a toy store and get a bull's head and a little lamb on wheels? Arrange them artistically, with a suitable background, and you will have a good cover." Whereupon he penciled on the tablecloth a rough sketch for a design, which was not only appropriate but highly striking. Suggestions of this kind stimulated our imaginations, and I believe that one of our most effective covers was that of a tiger, photographed direct in its natural colors from a beautiful $2000 rug that I happened to see in the shop window of a Broadway furrier. I had read the manuscript of the Lawson article the previous day, and as it contained the expression, "This cruel, tigerish, system," the beast's eyes, glaring at me through the glass, brought me to a halt, and in an instant gave me the idea.

On its business side, as well as in quality, "Everybody's Magazine" was created afresh during the first twelve months of our ownership. Abolishing the cut-price club plan, we put the subscription list on a stronger basis, and in a year doubled our circulation. As a natural result, we also doubled our advertising rate. When we bought the property, its price was $150 a page, one dollar per page per thousand circulation being the recognized rate among general magazines, though an extra twenty, or even fifty, thousand is often given for good measure.

With a showing of three hundred thousand we could ask $3oo a page, and on this healthy footing we already stood when the publication of '' Frenzied Finance'' began to increase our circulation to the merry tune of fifty thousand copies a month.

CHAPTER THIRTEEN
THE DISCOVERY OF TOM LAWSON

CHAPTER THIRTEEN

THE DISCOVERY OF TOM LAWSON

I T was as a private in a company of Hayes and Wheeler Cadets that I had my first glimpse of Thomas W. Lawson. That curious phase of our political life, the torchlight club, reached its climax of extravagance in the legion of plumed knights who eight years later went down to defeat with James G. Blaine, but it was a sprightly and picturesque factor in the Tilden-Hayes campaign, and as such served as a vent for the abundant energy of the youthful Lawson. I did not know him personally then, for he was a captain, and even in campaign clubs, captains and privates are far removed.

But I heard so much of him as we made our noisy crusades about the suburbs of Boston that his share in this boyish episode persisted in my memory till our actual acquaintance began.

In the twenty odd years which intervened, the captain of the torchlight company became a captain of finance. If a single word can summarize an epoch, the word for that quarter century is money. Colossal fortunes never rolled themselves up more quickly; men of commanding intellect never devoted themselves with more relentless energy to a sordid ideal. The ally of the foremost financiers, Thomas W. Lawson's knowledge of the inner history of this period was second to none, and when one day, disgusted with the methods of his associates, he told the press of America that he meant to spend the rest of his life — and his fortune if necessary — in showing up Standard Oil, our silent partner, Mr. Wilder, was struck with an idea. Dining with me that evening, he suggested that if we could get Tom Lawson to write the story of Amalgamated Copper for our magazine, we should have something worth telling, something people would be eager to read, something which would boom our circulation. The idea made an instant appeal to me, and the next morning I mentioned it to Ridgway, saying I approved of it, and that, if he agreed, I would attempt to secure the story. He replied that Wilder had telephoned him about it the day before, and that while he doubted if we could get it, he saw no harm in trying. That night, notwithstanding I had received no answer to a telegram inquiring whether Mr. Lawson was there, I went to Boston, taking with me the editor, John O'Hara Cosgrave.

As a preliminary move we first called on my friend, General Charles H. Taylor, of "The Boston Globe." It is not a matter of common knowledge that General Taylor was one of the pioneer ten-cent magazine publishers. Launching his venture under the name of "American Homes," he was on the threshold of a tremendous success when the great Boston fire of 1872-73 destroyed his editions and plant. But for this he would doubtless have set the pace for other magazines instead of concentrating his energy upon publishing the powerful daily so ably managed by his talented sons. Retaining a keen interest in the field where he himself had turned so promising a furrow, he readily gave me a letter of introduction, and as I have often known trifles to score where larger artillery fails, I thought it expedient to ask him to mention that, a Boston boy myself, I had once marched among Mr. Lawson's torchlight hosts. This General Taylor did, and, as Mr.

252

Lawson himself afterwards told me, the allusion reached its mark.

Our first attempt to see him, however, was unsuccessful, but his secretary told us that we had interested Mr. Lawson, who wished to know exactly the kind of articles we wanted and what we proposed to do about advertising them. Then, finally, at the close of the day, there was brought to our hotel a typewritten paragraph, unsigned, which stated that he knew just what we desired, but not being certain he wanted then to begin to write it, would give the matter consideration. With this showing, which might mean all or nothing, the editor and I returned to New York.

Now foremost among the personal characteristics of Mr. Cosgrave is the quality of persistence. He had assisted Doubleday-Page in editing "Everybody's" under the John Wanamaker regime, and coming over to us at the time we bought the property, was the acting editor of the magazine under Mr. Ridgway. He had already shown signs of the great ability which, on the establishment of "Ridgway's Weekly," later won him the full editorship of "Everybody's," at a salary equaled by few editors. At the time of which I write this dominant quality was even stronger, untempered by experience, than it is now, and in the hope that he might put our business in so plausible a light that Mr. Lawson would consent, we sent him back to Boston. It was without doubt his resolute siege of the financier's outer office which finally won, for after many days Mr. Lawson became so impressed with his persistence that he granted him an interview. This talk had its prompt sequel in a general conference which settled the matter on a basis beyond our rosiest dreams. In his characteristic manner Mr. Lawson outlined what he hoped to accom-

254

plish, disclosed his remedy for the evils he proposed to attack, and then stating that having looked us up since our first request for an interview and decided that we were game, told us that he intended to write the articles for serial publication without payment, and to advertise them in the daily newspapers at his own expense. We had secured a prize unique in the annals of magazine publishing.

But where, it was often asked, did Lawson come in? There was no ready answer to the question, for we never precisely knew. "The Remedy," which he explained to us at our second interview, was only to be given to the public after "Frenzied Finance" was finished. It was his belief that when this was unfolded and the American people, with the great downfall of the trusts, had come into possession of the millions ruthlessly pillaged from them, he also, in common with the people,

255

would reap the material benefit of his work.

The profit to "Everybody's" was happily less remote. Mr. Lawson's first article sketched, in his inimitable way, what he meant to tell. The *hors-d'œuvres* of the feast to follow, it whetted the appetite of the American public as never did cocktail and caviar tempt the palate of the veriest gourmet. Nor did Jonah open wider eyes upon his record-breaking gourd than we turned on the miracle wrought in our circulation. We beheld the wonderful vision of owning a great magazine property without the long, hard preparatory struggle of a "Munsey" or a "McClure"; we saw ourselves, free of worry as to personal needs, possessed of power to continue our work for what we believed to be the common good.

Mr. Lawson's laurels were not to pass unchallenged, however. The July issue, wherein "Frenzied Finance" began its spectacular career, also contained the first installment of a serial which we had arranged to publish long before the Lawson project arose. In the early autumn Mr. Hall Caine performed his annual pilgrimage to London to call upon his publisher. The latter, having transatlantic connections, mentioned to the author that the circulation of "Everybody's Magazine" had made extraordinary gains. "Yes," said Mr. Caine, "I expected it. That is the American magazine which is publishing my new story, 'The Prodigal Son.'"

It was my lot to have many interviews with our remarkable contributor, some of them intensely interesting. Indeed, I may say that although I have waited hours, even days, to see him — so many were the demands upon his time — I have always felt repaid for the delay. A fluent talker, his conversation was as entertaining as

257

his literary style, which I need remind
no one has a racy vigor all its own.
These visits of mine had mainly to do
with the exploiting of "Frenzied Finance."
At the time he promised us the story we
had discussed many suggestions for its
advertisement. One was that we offer
$50,000 as a prize for the best essay on
"Frenzied Finance" at the end of its
serial run. As Mr. Lawson put this forward as the condition on which he would
give us his story, we readily assented,
though we believed and eventually persuaded him, that there were more effective
ways of advertising. The regular monthly
announcements each involved a race against
time. Magazine publishers usually send out
the advertisements of their forthcoming
issue in advance, the agent mailing them
direct to the newspapers with instructions
to insert on the day of publication. It
was never possible for us to follow this

258

custom. Written by Mr. Lawson the afternoon before the magazine was to appear,
the advertisements of "Frenzied Finance"
were put in type by some Boston newspaper and then rushed to the other dailies
throughout the country by telegraph.
Once in a while the announcement would
be ready in time for someone to carry it
to New York, whence it could be telephoned to nearer points, like Philadelphia,
Baltimore, and Washington. But these
occasions for economy were rare.

Joining him late one afternoon for a
twelfth hour consultation of this sort, I
found his desk heaped high with a mass
of letters, telegrams, and checks, all in
answer to one of his large financial advertisements of the day before. He was
forming a $5,000,000 pool for the pur-
pose of selling short American Smelt-
ing and certain other stocks which he
claimed were grossly inflated. By the

action of this pool these stocks were to be put down to a point near their real value. Only wealthy men were invited to participate, and the smallest check acceptable from any one person was $25,000. Taking up one of these letters, with its lemon-colored enclosure, he turned it over to me with the remark, "That's a good-sized check, Thayer." The amount was $50,000; the letter, which began "Dear Tom," said briefly that the writer believed in the pool and would later in the week, perhaps, double his subscription. Both letter and check were signed "Russell Sage." Since the venerable financier had been handled without gloves in his articles, I was surprised, but as the check also bore the usual scrawl of a bank cashier, it did not occur to me to doubt its authenticity. A few days later, however, happening to call on the vice-president of the Corn Exchange Bank, upon which the check was drawn.

I asked to see their method of certification, and then perceived that the $5,000,000 pool was short a distinguished member. When I next saw Mr. Lawson I told him that he had deliberately deceived me. The wonder in his blue eyes turned to merriment as I explained. "That was fair," he said. "It was sent me as a joke — I passed it on."

During one of my trips to New England I chanced to be a witness of his sensational meeting with the mining operator, Colonel Greene. The latter, using page advertisements in the daily press, had called the author of "Frenzied Finance" a liar, a fakir, and a charlatan, and stated that he proposed to take an early train to Boston to settle with him. On the appearance of this advertisement, we received a telegram from a city in the far West, addressed to Mr. Lawson. It ran: "Bully boy. You are doing a great work. Others besides

Colonel Greene have notches in their guns. I am taking first train to Boston." I also took the first train to Boston, in the hope that I might arrive in advance of these two redoubtable warriors. In the morning papers that day appeared a telegram, supposedly from Mr. Lawson to Colonel Greene, to the effect that as he had much consideration for his office, which contained many art treasures, he would meet him in front of the Old State House, where the blood of patriots had previously been shed. Crowds thronged the historic spot, but Colonel Greene failed to appear. On my way to Mr. Lawson's home that evening, he regaled me with a number of interesting episodes of his earlier life, wherein attempts to assassinate him had proved futile. Securing lodging for the night at the Touraine, the clerk telephoned me early the next morning that Mr. Lawson had called and sent in his card to Colonel

Greene, who by now had reached the battleground. Hastily donning my clothes, and without breakfast, I descended just in time to witness their meeting in the hotel corridor, and to mount with them to Colonel Greene's apartments. No weapons were used in this encounter. It was a battle of words, in which the author of "Frenzied Finance" was an easy victor.

At this period Mr. Lawson figured in an episode closely personal to myself. I have referred in an earlier chapter to the touching tribute paid me by my friends when I left Philadelphia. It remained a warm memory in the years which followed, and I cherished the hope that I might some day show my appreciation. In January, 1905, this thought of a decade crystallized in a definite plan. I decided that I would myself give a dinner and ask, not only those old-time friends, but such new ones as had in the meantime come upon my horizon.

263

Public dinners are often stupid affairs, and unless a Patrick Francis Murphy or a Simeon Ford is to speak, they are avoided by the man fond of home and family. Private dinners, without some amusing feature, may be quite as uninteresting, and I therefore planned that my guests should be entertained in some novel way. Given under such circumstances, no representatives of the press were permitted to be present. Nevertheless, the newspapers of New York and other cities printed various accounts. The one which follows has its humorous points:

LAWSON OF BOSTON BRINGS PROSPERITY TO MAGAZINE

Publisher of "Frenzied Finance" Series Gives Dinner at St. Regis, on Gold Plates — Lawson Talks over Phone

"NEW YORK, February 20 — (Special) John Adams Thayer, who is Secretary and Treasurer of the Ridgway-Thayer Publishing Company, gave a dinner at the St. Regis Hotel to-night to celebrate his birthday anniversary. Incidentally the dinner also celebrated the prosperity of 'Everybody's Magazine' since it became the medium through which Thomas W. Lawson of Boston exposes himself and others.

"It was a feast fit to celebrate a six months' hunt for the money devil. About Thayer sat nearly forty congratulants. Some of them share his present prosperity, but most of them are men with whom he had been associated in the past. They had been invited with cards which were engraved in facsimile of Thayer's own handwriting. As a cheerful jest they had also been furnished with cards entitling them to admission at the front entrance of the St. Regis.

"The dinner was served on a modest

265

collection of plate which the hotel classifies as its 'special banquet gold service.' The menus were bound in brown leather, and included a letter from Lawson to Thayer, which carefully was copyrighted by Thayer, thus keeping it from any possibility of reproduction by vulgar newspapers.

"Telephones had been provided at the place of each guest, and at ten o'clock the inevitable Thomas Lawson, who is in Boston, was put into connection with all of them at once. He talked for twenty minutes. Some of his auditors said afterward it wouldn't do at all for them to tell what he said. Others said simply they couldn't remember.

"Certainly Lawson dealt cheerfully with the host of the evening, and complimented him on his prosperity in battling with the armies of greed and their vulgar display of ill-gotten wealth. Likewise, he said the past, present, and future finance was

266

known only to one man, and that one man was at the Boston end of the telephone."

Mr. Lawson's speech by telephone was not at all serious. His letter, on the other hand, struck a different note, yet one equally characteristic of the man. It was entitled "Looping the Life Circle," and was read by Mr. Ridgway, who has oratorical abilities of no mean order. Copyrighted as it was at the time, it has never before been published.

"Looping the life circle is the order of human existence. Old Ringmaster Time cracks his whip as the man steps out upon the flying zone to begin his wonderful journey by way of sunland, moon, and starland to the enchanted chamber at the world's end. Round the great orbit he swings through spring days and summertime, and above the music of the spheres the crack of the Ringmaster's whip signals the passing years, faintly at first, louder as the mellow autumn shadows fall and in thunder tones as the circle spins into the hoary regions where Winter is king. To-night the echo of the whip's crack, dimly heard, is in the air, and we who cling near your rim of the circle rejoice that its course is still in the August loop, and that before you and us stretch glorious days of racing in space amid suns and constellations hung out for our delectation. Afar off, indefinite as a dream, is the enchanted chamber, so that what need we care, while our grip on the rim is strong, for the lightning play or the bleak wind that blows in the wild waste places, or for the gray gatesman at the world's end. To-night's flight is through the perfume of stellar gardens; to-morrow we will pick the ripened fruit in Orion's orchards, and before Time's whip cracks out again, who knows through

what Aladdin realm we may be flitting.
So let us be glad — glad of the speed and
the beauty, of the perfume and the vision,
but most of all glad that Fate has set us
so close together on the circle rim that
while the echo of the Ringmaster's whip
is still in the air, we can clasp each other's
hands and know that whatever storms lower,
we have not to weather them alone."

I possess two personally inscribed books
of Mr. Lawson's. One is "The Lawson
History of the America's Cup," the other
"Frenzied Finance." In the latter he
penned this:

"My dear Thayer, — As sure as water
seeks its level, released balloons the sky,
and stocks the earth, crime will hunt
its creator.

"You little thought when General Taylor
sent you with that note that you and I
would be condemned to travel hell together

without a fire extinguisher or insurance policy, but we live and learn.

"To show you I do, and that I pick blooms from the bush of forgiveness as I travel, I wish you and yours a most happy Christmas. Believe me,

"Yours very truly,

"THOMAS W. LAWSON.

"Boston, December 25, 1905."

CHAPTER FOURTEEN

DIVORCED — WITH ALIMONY

CHAPTER FOURTEEN

DIVORCED — WITH ALIMONY

MR. LAWSON'S great serial began its course in July, and as it is customary to give the cover design of that month a patriotic touch, this issue, the best we could produce, bore an eagle with outspread wings and the American flag printed in strong colors. The red, white, and blue attracted much attention on the news-stands. It also drew the notice of the Chief Police Commissioner of Boston, who declared that the American flag was used as an advertisement, and that therefore the magazine could not be sold. The newsdealers in Boston, however, always ready for an emergency, decided that their customers should be supplied, even without the covers, and so announced by large signs. Whereupon the Commissioner's decision, of course, got into the newspapers, whose many comments and editorials led to increased sales in Boston and vicinity. Perceiving a chance to help the sales in other parts of the country, I made a hurried trip to Boston and had a talk with the Commissioner. He had a charming personality and was very polite, but insisted that he must obey the letter of the law and prohibit the sale of the magazine. After my talk with him I gave an interview to the Boston papers, told of the conference, and stated that the publishers of "Everybody's Magazine" had no thought of desecrating the American flag—in fact, that we did not consider the cover an advertisement at all. Our idea was to encourage rather than to discourage patriotism. Changing

274

the cover of the second edition, which was then on the presses, we reproduced in a large broadside many of the editorials and items referring to the suppression of the first edition, and sent these sheets to the editors of newspapers throughout the country, requesting them, as believers in right and justice, to reprint some of them, with or without comment. The fact that we were ourselves large advertisers at the time helped considerably, and the immense amount of free advertising which we received resulted in the sale of the second edition. In many places throughout the country copies of the July issue were sold at three and four times its regular price, and extraordinary stories reached us of the manner in which the magazine circulated from hand to hand. In a letter which came to us from an isolated town near Quebec, it was stated that one copy of the July issue had been read by forty-five different people.

Then began the incessant call for back numbers. The demand was so great that we printed a little pamphlet called "The Chapters Which Went Before," and this assisted greatly in putting the story in the hands of the public. Although the August issue exceeded its predecessor by fifty thousand copies, it yet fell twenty-five thousand short of the newsdealers' requirements. Month by month we taxed the full capacity of a number of printing establishments, until, in less than a year after Mr. Lawson's articles began, we announced an edition of one million, which he himself had predicted.

In the meantime we had to effect a revolution in our advertising. With our circulation climbing in the amazing fashion I have described, we justly felt that our price for advertising should increase pro rata, but as it is customary for publishers to give notice of an advance, meanwhile taking orders at the old rate for a year, we found ourselves in a dilemma. The unusual situation seemed to warrant unusual measures, and we accordingly decided to break with tradition and announce an immediate increase, without notice, to $400 per page. To impress advertisers with the fact that the occasion was exceptional in every way, we printed this announcement in two colors on Japanese parchment paper, and giving it the form of a proclamation, affixed the signature of the secretary and the seal of the company at the bottom. Yet even before a later rate of $500 per page was established, our circulation had so grown that we felt certain of an ultimate monthly issue of a million. We thereupon made a price of a dollar a line per thousand circulation, with a bonus of one hundred thousand thrown in, but this device was short-lived. Advertisers must know in advance what they are to pay; otherwise it is impossible for them to arrange their expenditure.

These rapidly advancing prices made our back-cover page very costly, for this position in all magazines is valued at four times a regular page. It so happened that one of these back covers was for once not sold in advance. A week remained in which to find a customer at its fixed price; I was in a quandary. We had announced an edition of a million copies, and this space, which at the old rate had brought as high as $2000, had now doubled in value. Who would buy a page worth $4000? Then I had an inspiration. Why not advertise it! Such a thing had never been done, but if anything of value could be sold by advertising, why not this? The idea came to me in the early morning — at the hour when dreams come — and it was so realistic that I awoke, rose, and wrote the announcement. Then I sought repose again and found it. I also found a buyer for the page. On the very day of its appearance in the morning "Sun" my advertisement brought a customer.

The problems of the immediate hour were so exacting that it was impossible to attempt many innovations in my special province. One favorite project I could not carry out aimed to group our advertising in departments which should each be prefaced by a few pages of reading matter. I did, however, introduce a "Classified Advertising Department," consisting of small announcements. This was a new feature for a monthly, notwithstanding the fact that "The Outlook," a very successful weekly, had inserted pages of small advertisements for many years. This idea proved so popular — some sixteen pages appearing in the early numbers — that

279

other magazines followed our lead, to the profit of themselves and their clients alike. Our contemporaries also paid us the compliment of borrowing the "Index to Advertisements," which the remarkable bulk and range of our announcements caused me to inaugurate.

Those were roaring times in the advertising world generally, and what with the growth of the field and the dearth of specialists, I had presently to pay $15,000 annually, with a contract for three years, to the wonderfully efficient man who took the burden of "Everybody's" advertising department off my shoulders.

Giving our readers the same number of reading pages as "Harper's" and "The Century," we felt that we were entitled to more than ten cents a copy. But to raise the subscription price of a magazine is an important step. I was well aware of this, for "The Ladies' Home Journal" had doubled its price a few years before I went to it, and I had specially studied the working of this phase of publishing. With our mounting circulation and low advertising rate, for the higher prices, though announced, were not yet in force, profits were small. At fifteen cents a copy there would be little loss on circulation. When to make the change was the problem. Then one morning the daily newspapers did us the kindness to print the statement that "Everybody's Magazine" was to be suppressed. The attorney for Henry H. Rogers, of Standard Oil fame, had written the American News Company that if the magazines were distributed and put on sale throughout the country, action at law would be taken. The elevated train on which I rode that morning seemed to creep at a snail's pace. Arriving at my office, I burst in on Mr. Ridgway.

"Now's the time!" I cried.

With the dignity of a foreign ambassador, the active partner of my troubles leaned back in his chair and smiled.

" Yes ; for what ? " said he.

" To increase our price ! "

My co-worker took fire himself. In a moment he had our printer on the telephone, the presses were stopped, and the change was made. The free advertising given us by the magic name of Standard Oil was so immense that the edition for the month, though larger than before, was swept from the news-stands on the day of publication.

Our horizon was sometimes troubled with clouds without this silver lining of gratuitous advertisement. We never worried about the money for the payroll or for the paper or for the printer — those nightmares which haunt the bedsides of many publishers ; but we did face breathtaking situations. These were more or less closely related to Mr. Lawson's personality. One such episode had its storm center in a picture of Mr. J. Pierpont Morgan, to whom Mr. Lawson referred in one of his chapters. Not finding a good photograph for reproduction, we asked Mr. Lawson if he had one we might use, with the upshot that we made a plate from a steel engraving which was in itself a work of art. After the magazine appeared on the news-stands we were waited upon at our offices by the publisher of the engraving — a limited edition — and he came prepared. He had with him, in fact, the law of copyright, which clearly stated that one dollar a copy could be claimed for every impression we had made. Inasmuch as our output that month totalled seven hundred thousand copies, we were liable for $700,000. It was a most interesting afternoon.

Another incident, as disconcerting,

283

reached its climax while we were preparing to issue "Frenzied Finance" in book form. Literary friends of Mr. Lawson had advised him that his material should be rearranged for book publication, and to this he agreed. At the last moment, however, by a quick decision of the author, it was all restored to the original shape in which it had appeared in the magazine. As we were very anxious to publish the first volume promptly, this embarrassed us, but we pushed the work forward, and having more than half the book in type, were pluming ourselves on our wonderful progress, when Mr. Lawson again called a halt with a long telegram. Our dismay may be imagined as we read that he preferred another style of type and that the book must be reset. He added that it was one of his constitutional proclivities to change things, and referred us to a certain remark made by District

284

Attorney Jerome at a public dinner in Kansas City. On this occasion, which was in Mr. Lawson's honor, Mr. Ridgway had used this language: "When God needed a father of his country, He raised a Washington; when He needed an emancipator for the country, He raised a Lincoln; when He needed a savior of the country, He raised a Lawson." Mr. Jerome, who followed, paraphrased this dizzy flight by saying that, in his opinion, when God created Lawson He needed someone to raise hell.

The close of "Frenzied Finance" found us issuing between five and six hundred thousand copies monthly. Long before this we had striven to produce a magazine which, outside the Lawson feature, should be well worth its price, and hence it fell out that the great bulk of the circulation was retained. With an increased advertising income, not only were dividends in order, but also larger salaries. Visions came of owning my own home and an automobile or two. The magazine was on such a sound footing that it would take years of mismanagement or extravagant expenditure to injure the property. With the advertising department in the hands of a capable manager, I planned to travel extensively, taking turns with my partner. I even thought of going around the world. "See America first," was in my thought, however, and soon a trip was made to California. I dined at the Poodle Dog in San Francisco, fished at Catalina Island, saw the Grand Cañon of Arizona, spent a delightful afternoon and evening with Professor John Muir on the edge of the Petrified Forest, and returned in Mr. Wilder's private car to New York. I had been gone two months. During my absence ambitious plans for the establishment of a weekly paper had been hatched by Mr.

Ridgway. It was to be a great national journal, published under the name of " Ridgway's — A Militant Weekly for God and Country." As big locally as nationally, it was to be published in fourteen of the largest cities of the country, with responsible heads and assistants in each city. The Washington Bureau was to be the great important feature. The people were to be told exactly what the Government was doing with the thousand millions of dollars it spends every year. In this city alone a staff of from six to ten newsgatherers and editors would garner the week's history and telegraph it on Friday to each of the cities where " Ridgway's" was to appear. Moreover, it was to have, the Foreword stated, good wholesome fiction, with honest sentiment and " red blood."

I was not in sympathy with this grandiose dream. I had risked my all at the establishment of " Everybody's," and now that we were out of debt, I wanted to see a surplus before I gave serious thought to another publication. I therefore advised my partner to put it aside for another year or two till we should be in a better position to take it up. Surprised as I was at his determination not to delay the founding of his weekly, I was still more taken aback when the project was seconded by our silent partner. Mr. Wilder, during our business life, sat as judge upon our differences, which were few and far between, and in this instance I felt as confident as I had on the other occasions that he would decide with me. I found myself in the minority, however. Their idea was another ''engine fighting for the common good.'' In my own life I had fought long and hard for my daily bread, and before taking up the fight for others on this colossal scale, I wanted to see myself so entrenched that I need not worry about personal needs. I was between the upper and nether millstones. One of my partners was blessed as few men are blessed, and in addition had much of this world's goods. Mr. Ridgway had his interest in the magazine and the ambition to plant his Excelsior flag on loftier heights. Divorce, therefore, was the natural outcome, and it came quickly. Disposing of the larger part of my interest at a price which was considered fair, my alimony was further swelled by the continuance of my salary for three years. S. S. McClure and John S. Phillips, of "McClure's Magazine," parted company about the same time, but the sentiment which attended the break between these college chums and intimate friends played no part in my separation from Mr. Ridgway. We were merely co-workers for three happy years of business life. To Mr. Wilder I was bound by other ties.

289

Since then water has flowed under the bridge. The weekly I opposed long since completed its short cycle from premature birth to early death. Its nineteen numbers entailed a loss of over $300,000! But "Everybody's," soundly based, has gone on from strength to strength. Even as I end this chapter the newspapers tell me that, by increasing its stock by three millions, the Butterick Company has acquired "Everybody's Magazine." Three millions of Butterick stock for the publication we bought in 1903 for $75,000! And it is worth it — even more.

Since then, also, I have enjoyed to the full the vacation I have earned. The reader who has followed these pages to their close — my companion for thirty-five years — will realize what this has meant to me. I have looked upon men and cities. I have circled the globe. And, indeed, it is a small globe. Even in India my eyes fell upon the hoary advertisement, "Mother Almost Gave Up Hope," and as I recognized one after another familiar nostrum, exiled from its native land, I perceived that the heathen in his blindness bows down to more than wood and stone.

In this holiday of mine there comes to me every now and then that sage warning of my old-time friend: "Don't get in a rut." Recalling this, I think of men who have retired temporarily from business, only to lose all desire to resume their share in the world's work. Then I ask myself if this happy, do-as-you-please life is growing on me. Am I becoming a chronic pleasure-seeker? Am I falling into a vacation rut? And I say to myself: "Look out!"

INDEX

INDEX

295

298